VAGABONDING

CHRISTINA THÜRMER-ROHR

Translated by Lise Weil

VAGABONDING

FEMINIST THINKING CUT LOOSE

Beacon Press
Boston

Beacon Press
25 Beacon Street
Boston, Massachusetts 02108

Beacon Press Books are published
under the auspices of
the Unitarian Universalist Association of Congregations.

98 97 96 95 94 93 92 91   8 7 6 5 4 3 2 1

Published by arrangement with
Orlanda Frauenverlag, Berlin.

Text design by
Douglass G. A. Scott

Library of Congress Cataloging-in-Publication Data
Thürmer-Rohr, Christina.
[Vagabundinnen. English]
Vagabonding: feminist thinking cut loose /
Christina Thürmer-Rohr; translated by Lise Weil.
p.   cm.
Translation of: Vagabundinnen.
Includes bibliographical references.
ISBN 0-8070-6756-3
1. Feminism.   2. Human ecology.   3. Feminist criticism.
I. Title.
HQ1154.T48   1991
305.42—dc20   90-21575   CIP

CONTENTS

ACKNOWLEDGMENTS

I would like to thank Claudia Koppert for supporting this book in its early stages and for her care and help in working on the manuscript; all the students in the women's studies program at the Institute for Social Pedagogy at the Technical University of Berlin and my colleague Carola Wildt for their inspirational collaboration; and my fourteen-year-old son, Til, for his understanding and helpfulness.

TRANSLATOR'S INTRODUCTION

This collection of essays emerges from a decade of unprecedented environmental disaster, a decade of events which has made visible as never before the enormity of the threat to life on this earth posed by the human beings living on it. It offers an unblinking and unrelieved account not only of the monstrous facts that surround and condition human existence at the end of this twentieth century – but also of what these facts tell us about the human creatures, men and women, who have collectively brought them into being.

Vagabonding is by any account a grim book – yet the fact is that on my first reading of it, in two breathless sessions near the end of a summer of intense heat and drought here in the northeastern United States, the feeling of relief was so powerful it brought on tears. I was forced to realize how hard I had been trying not to take in the evidence all around: the swatch of forest suddenly gone, a bulldozer in its place, a metal frame going up, oversized, hideous, never to be reconciled with its site . . . the eerie glare of the sun; the way it used to burn, and now it was *biting*. Reading Thürmer-Rohr's essays that summer the censors were suddenly routed; I allowed myself to feel it, to say it to myself with all the force of unleashed knowing: that something has gone unspeakably wrong, that we human beings have made a terminal mess of this earth, that there is no certainty we will redeem it or ourselves.

Vagabonding is, of course, not unique in attempting to

break through our walls of denial about the dangers we face at this time in history. This past decade has given rise to an avalanche of books and articles with apocalyptic titles and dire messages. Almost always, though, the price of clear-sightedness about the nuclear peril or the environmental crisis is the erasure of men's specific role in these disasters. Most writers, if they search for explanations at all, are content to deal in abstractions and universals like "civilization," "human nature," or "the nature of matter." Thürmer-Rohr, to her great credit, never shrinks from naming the perpetrators of this mess: it is men, specifically white men from Western nations, who have brought us to the brink of ecological holocaust and nuclear annihilation. (At the same time, I suspect that it is in women's bodies, especially, that the knowledge of this poisoning is stored, that it accumulates steadily . . . then has to be tamped down just so we can get on with our lives.) And so for women – and it is women Thürmer-Rohr is primarily addressing in this book – the choice is clear: we must stop saying yes to these men and their projects, their constructions and inventions.

It was feminist thinkers of the Second Wave in this country – foremost among them Mary Daly – who led the way in uncovering and denouncing what five thousand years of male rule have done to women and to the earth. Thürmer-Rohr's thinking is grounded in the insights of these thinkers, who insist on tracing the critical ills of this time back to their roots in patriarchal domination. Yet her thinking is also strikingly distinct from theirs. For one thing, as a European living with an acute and daily awareness of chemical and nuclear contamination such as few of us can imagine in this country, and as a West German living in Berlin, a city with a strong military presence and borders defined by barbed wire and nuclear warheads, she is necessarily critical of utopian leanings – and skeptical of any notion of a free field for feminist thought and creation. (The events of November 1989 and their aftermath have as yet not substantially altered any of these facts, except for the barbed wire.) As unflinching as she is in her condemnation of the Western male and his violent and destructive history, she refuses in these essays to see women as categorically divorced from this history. In fact, Thürmer-Rohr insists, we are necessarily implicated in it. Women may have stood outside the corridors of power – we have not, we could not have, stood outside of patriarchy. Nor can we do so now.

If Thürmer-Rohr's relationship to feminism is often ambivalent, it is largely because her prime commitment is to the free range of the mind, not only in the sense of taking all of history as her arena, but also of cutting loose from all attachments. The kind of movement she urges on women is one that "sees the familiar only as an occasion to leave false homes again, which is *not* in search of 'identity,' that idée fixe." The essence of "vagabonding" as a way of life, and as a way of knowing, is to fight every "thought prohibition" that stands in its way, even when that prohibition comes from feminist quarters. Thus Thürmer-Rohr has been bold enough to assert that women have been *complicit* in men's crimes against them and the earth, for without our participation men could not have carried out these crimes. Women have been expert at passivity, at forgiveness, at reconciliation, at averting our eyes. If we haven't outright supported men, then we've done nothing to prevent them from fouling the earth. It is for this notion of female complicity – *Mittäterschaft*

– that Thürmer-Rohr, a professor of Women's Studies and
one-time pianist in a women's rock band, has become a much
discussed and controversial figure among feminists in Europe.
We feminists, while critical of the construct of
"woman," have not always managed to avoid the pitfalls of
feminine behavior and thinking – when, for example, on the
basis of our special powers as women, we assign to ourselves
the task of cleaning up the mess men have made, of setting
a moral example, or saving the planet. As far as radical
feminism has gone in the direction of deconstructing male
history and thought, we have not always been able to resist
filling the space that thus opens up to us with our own
dreams, desires, hopes. Thürmer-Rohr would have us resist
this temptation, would have us occupy this empty space with
no preconceptions, no prescriptions, no ideals.

Of the many objections that have been raised to *Vagabonding* in the years since it first appeared in Germany –
including the most obvious one, that it indulges in "blaming
the victim" – most are anticipated and answered by the
essays themselves. To my mind the most compelling of these
objections is that the author's emphasis on women's shared
role in patriarchal history effectively erases the fact of lesbian
presence and the existence of lesbian community.* Indeed,
no mention of lesbians is to be found in any of the essays.
This is a curious omission in light of the fact that lesbians
have so often defined themselves in distinct opposition to
the category of "woman" and all the characteristics Thürmer-

* Lena Laps, "Wir sind die Lesben, auf die wir gewartet haben," *Ihrsinn 1*, pp.
37–38. Related concerns are raised in Maria Zemp's unpublished paper, "Ohne
Hoffnung Kein Politik" (1988).

Rohr assigns to it: orientation to men and male interests, loyalty to the male order, sex-role complementarity, and general complacency about the destructiveness of the male sex.

Thürmer-Rohr seems to be anticipating such an objection when she suggests, in the last essay of the book, that those who choose to leave the false homes at men's side to create new ones are condemned to repeat the past. That she is suspicious of identification with lesbians and lesbian community, especially if couched in even faintly anointed terms, is entirely consistent with Thürmer-Rohr's anti-utopian orientation, her skepticism about the possibility of female autonomy, and her mistrust of the search for "identity." Still, a way of life among women which has persisted throughout history as an alternative to patriarchal society, and which, in Europe and North America, exercised particular political force in the very decade in which she situates her essays, ought, it seems to me, to have received some positive acknowledgment in this book.

Vagabonding offers us nowhere to stand and no hope with which to stand there. Instead it gives us, in the author's own words, a "fury of questions," the rage of a woman trying to cut through the fog of deception and denial, to shake us, and herself, into vibrant awareness, into *feeling*. If this in itself does not inspire hope, it may inspire women with the courage to occupy this empty space before us as we have never done or been asked to do – our minds ranging far and wide and fiercely, daring to enter forbidden places, not getting stuck anywhere. For there are, Thürmer-Rohr insists, worse things even than the end of life on earth: "I do not love this existence in its mere biological definition enough to see the possible human-made finale as the *greatest* catastrophe. I see as even greater the catastrophe of wasting, in the time remaining to us, our possibilities as women with *this* history and in *this* present, of throwing them away, of sleeping through them, that is, of falling behind ourselves."

Thanks to Beacon editors Marya E. Van't Hul and Deborah Johnson for sensitive and inspired collaboration on this translation.

AUTHOR'S PREFACE

The texts collected here were written between 1983 and 1987, between the so-called *Nachrüstungsdebatte,* Chernobyl, and the German elections of 1987.

It is a time in which both the noxiousness and the banality of male society have become all but indescribable. On the one hand, you must have a very high pain threshold not to erect safety zones around yourself in self-defense. On the other hand, this time forces me to come closer to reality. Thus, these writings are the expression not only of despair at the worthlessness and self-defilement of this male culture, but also of a fury of questions, a fury that arises when I give up my ordered way of seeing. It is not that my "identity" becomes questionable – it has been for a long time; it's not that I become homeless – I have been for quite a while; I *am* without an ideal of self and I know it. The setting, the framework, has shattered.

Women cannot surround themselves with overpowering models as men still do. Out of need or choice, men allow themselves the duty, and the pleasure, of submitting from time to time to the authority of another man; or they wander polyculturally through the world, on foot or in their heads, at once restless and calm, always stumbling upon something or rediscovering something in which they think they've found themselves or see themselves mirrored.[1] The rootlessness of these "free spirits," these sovereign recluses, is not the same as being homeless. Their world sits waiting for them, whether they scorn it or revere it, whether they approach it or leave it to itself.

"I don't need a home, I need freedom," says Peter Bichsel; "if that's guaranteed, then I'll find all the home I need, my wife, my girlfriend, Beethoven, Schubert, Lester Young, Tom Waits . . . Goethe and Robert Walser, Bakunin and Heinrich Heine, a drunk at the train station café."[2] To speak this way is possible only for someone who finds himself reflected everywhere in the world, for whom everything is at his disposal, as long as he's not nailed down and fenced in, as long as he's set free in his world: women, culture, and every corner of it.

On the whole, women know no such thing. To "leave the inner realm and move outside to the great scenes, outdoors, on the streets, abroad," this kind of freedom leads women into mirrorless space, not to experiences of self-discovery, scarcely to places of memory.[3] For in this freedom – of thought, of movement, of impulse – we do not find ourselves.

This is exactly the adventure that still excites and inspires: *not* to want to keep meeting yourself; to find out what it's like to walk around and think like a stranger, to be a stranger in knowledge; not to seek out those regions that fix us in repetition. To become knowledgeable in a world which intended to exclude women from knowledge.

By being "outside" I don't mean being on the road, where in the late twenties a hundred thousand men wandered – the unemployed and the adventurers, the rundown and the dropouts, the last descendants of the itinerant craftsmen and the modern hunger army of the Great Depression. These roving rebels, despite their mostly enforced but sometimes

elected poverty, aroused feelings which lent a certain popu-
larity to the homeless and those living on the edge, the social
defectors, especially in the eyes of artists and intellectuals.
These brothers of the highway saw themselves as outside
society and yet not so much homeless as at home on the
whole earth, with their brothers the trees and grass, animals
and humans; they intended their brotherhood to grow into
the great family of mankind.[4]

But "outside" for women is neither the symbolic road
– what would it be today, a superhighway or a shopping
mall? – nor the landscape of adventure and misery that on
the whole still seemed to offer a "home" and "family" for
men.

Whereas a man's longing is always a kind of homesickness, in which he remembers past happiness and searches for
something he once had that has since been destroyed, my
longing remains empty of images, without past or future
assurances.[5] Vagabonding is the symbol for a way of life
which does *not* latch on to the familiar, which sees the familiar
only as an occasion to leave false homes again, which is *not*
in search of "identity," that idée fixe.[6] It is a cure for the
kind of empathy which makes judgments impossible – in
other words, not letting myself get hooked. A path between
exhaustion and curiosity. A different kind of love of life.

Berlin
January 1987

VAGABONDING

1

THE END OF
CERTAINTY

In the fifties – after war and postwar experiences that cut deep but were accepted as fateful normalcy – I was confronted for the first time with the proliferation and the effects of nuclear weaponry, and with the debate over the nuclear arming of Germany. At that time, one thing was clear to me: the catastrophe will happen, and hopefully soon. I was convinced of the coming nuclear war and the imminent and total annihilation of human beings by human beings. Before I had really begun my life, I was willing to let it go, willing to recognize that life can't be clung to. To accept what humans have wrought as fate, to treat war as a religion requiring self-sacrifice, seemed a natural way of thinking.

This was not fear of the catastrophe, not despair and sorrow over the supposed absence of a future, not fearful anticipation of the end. The nihilistic conviction that human beings are meaningless, that life itself is meaningless, had taken on material form. Nuclear self-destruction was its logical expression, evidence of the absurdity of believing that human existence had meaning and purpose. There was no rebellion here, no pathos of despair, of hopelessness. It was a fatalism for which all-out war appeared as both occasion and solution: weariness with life, the secret weariness of ill-used human beings on this ill-used earth, of having to furnish life with long-term meaning.

My eager grasp at a vision of a quick and violent end was not, however, that of a would-be suicide. There was still something to seek in the world. Life was still *about* something – but in time-lapse. It was about more than simply existing. The time remaining was filled with endless expectations, with dissipation and overexertion, with the feeling of limitless freedoms and the courage to realize the utter lack of a future. Nothing had to be built, secured, preserved, clung to. This short life was a boon, a senseless luxury, a senseless passion – with no time for the inessential, the arbitrary, the indirect, the half-baked; with no room for the everyday. They were eliminated from this way of life. They interfered. They formed an unbearable contrast to the restless flights of the mind. They represented inauthentic life, and the unavoidability of this ordinariness caused more despair than knowing that authentic life could not in the long run be lived. This authentic life was governed by an indignant refusal of distractions and an absolute intolerance of all attempts from the outside to restrict our own ideas about life, or to regulate them through disciplinary action.

In 1955, when I was eighteen, I read *Death in Venice*. In the now slightly yellowed Fischer paperback with its typical fifties cover design, the marks of my selective fascination with this material of Thomas Mann's are still visible: vigorous pencil underlinings of phrases like "advantages of chaos," "obscenity and frenzy of decline," "sympathy with the abyss."[1]

The death-dealing epidemic on his trail, spreading secretly and relentlessly through the dirty alleyways of Venice, succeeded in undermining Gustav Aschenbach's regimen of bourgeois order – a regimen in which he had been, until now, prosperously and respectably settled. Against the background of decline, of imminent and certain decay, he took liberties which, in his life of steadfast manly dignity and in ignorance of his own desires, had never entered his mind; liberties which took him beyond the laws of art and of bourgeois reason. To expend one's energies unproductively in emotional intoxication, and for the love of a young boy – such a leap into the forbidden and out of social approbation and normalcy was possible only because Aschenbach expected death and not the continuation of life.

The pathos of life lived alongside death – when death is no longer banished from life into the realm of happenstance – makes one intolerant of thinking that persists in operating inside the limited dimensions of continuous progress. One becomes intolerant of spiritually diseased normalcy, of ordinariness, of any truncation of feelings, of time-wasting indifference. To live as if it's all over with the earth, one way or another, if not right away then soon, is excessive: it demands and expends everything at once. Such a way of life cannot wait for slow developments, has little patience, care, or consideration. It spares no one and saves nothing. It is irresponsible and formless; it has no morality, for it dismisses whatever fails to prove its worth – whatever disillusions. It has an affinity for illusion, for whether or not an experience is based on reality becomes immaterial. It is daring and is disgruntled at any acknowledgment of a reliable future. Conflicts are postponed, or if they can't be postponed, the pacifying solution is always the thought of general disintegration. There are no tasks, there is no agenda. The gaze narrows, focuses on sensations. There is nothing of importance to be discovered in everyday reality. And so what is frightening is not that it might cease, but rather that it might continue.

When one is convinced of the meaninglessness of human existence, one is not surprised that humanity is rigorously bringing this meaninglessness to an end, and one agrees with those who are doing so. Meanwhile, the systems of order flourishing in this meaninglessness are exposing themselves in all their absurdity.

The various images of humanity with which I have already tried to live are no longer tenable. I can no longer make sense of things apart from the fact that the atom bomb – like all other instruments of annihilation – is not a fate which descended on us from outside or from above. Rather, "The bomb [is] not a trace more evil than reality and not a hair more destructive than we are. It is merely our unfolding, a material representation of our essence. It is already embodied as a complete thing, whereas we are still relatively split. . . . The bomb demands of us – experience of the self. We are it. In it, the Western 'subject' fulfills itself."[2]

If I am to accept in the first place this "we" that does not differentiate between the powerful and the powerless, between men and women, if I thus assume that "we all" participate – albeit in very different functions – in the production of this symbol of civilized patriarchal thought, then the motive force behind any foreseeable future continues to be the existence of a factor of extermination that in forty years has increased a thousandfold and that continues to increase. The cynical provocation contained in this material image of the "human being" is staggering. It topples what remains of an image of humanity ennobled by hopes and utopias. What is at stake is the human being. The days of naivete, the days of defiant hopes, are over. My own innocence and that of those I would like to see as innocent is beyond recall. Whatever this is – shock, cynicism, despair, or repression – I feel it in my limbs, in my nerves, in my eyes, in the corners of my mouth, in my stomach.

To begin with, this robs the days of all cheerfulness. At one moment it's hatred that makes them dreary: disgust at those who call this defense-sadism a necessary form of self-preservation on the part of peoples and nations and who are in complacent agreement with this prevailing logic. These people are all around us and they are, as the last elections confirmed, the majority. To be sure, I do not feel as if I belong to them; in fact, I find them unbearable to the point of physical allergy – I avoid them, I avert my eyes and tune them out, I do not seek their company, I find other places to be.

Nevertheless I am enlightened enough to know that we, namely women, are not simply the "others." And so I don't hate only those who proceed as if nothing were wrong. I also struggle with self-contempt when I see myself grow hard, sullen, and cold, when I lose what allowed me to be joyful and kind: I see how I'm shrinking.

I had armed and protected myself with a kind of good faith and short-term view, equipped myself with life-sustaining errors. In all my partial or putative insight, in all my enlightened skepticism, I had not really expected the fulfillment of humanity's "evil" side.

With the development of the natural sciences in the nineteenth century, the idea that a higher purpose or a heavenly meaning directed human life on earth collapsed. And if God is dead, life appears blind, arbitrary, purposeless, lawless, dispensable, and irredeemable. What remains is only the world of nature, whose laws can be explained. The collapse of theological astronomy was a shock, a total loss of spiritual and emotional bearings – and not only for men.

Through their own discoveries, humans destroyed their own importance. Formerly "children of God," and godlike in their own eyes, they now became merely living creatures, neither indispensable nor unique, playthings of nonsense. Since then, humanity has been "moving ever faster . . . toward nothingness."[3] Who is the lawmaker, and who are the moral referees, if no god and no saints are dispensing justice and monitoring human actions? We are not meant to be, we simply are. Humans take revenge on all this meaninglessness by pursuing their own nothingness, by taking destruction into their own hands. This revenge, in which humans complete a logic that nature itself – despite its own lawfulness – stops short of completing, may be the only action they are still free to take.

Manufacturers, supporters, and tolerators of the bomb; the spread of nihilistic thinking that produced the mass mentality of the forties and fifties and the development of the instrument of mass annihilation; National Socialism as the first political movement to negate masses of people as people, in order to dispose of them like inanimate material or trash – all these formed a complex, and it seemed immaterial whether the existence of the bomb was proof of the meaninglessness of existence or the other way around: the meaninglessness of existence had become the legitimation for the existence of the bomb. We're not really here for any reason, the bomb will inevitably drop, and since the bomb is here, we're worthless anyway, and since we're worthless, the bomb can't make it any worse.

The meaninglessness of the world became linked to this conclusion: nothing matters, everything is allowed; whether the world exists or not is all the same. So it might just as well not exist, so there's no reason not to destroy it; so there's also no reason not to agree to its destruction.

Recently, the 1979 NATO arms resolution stirred memories of such thoughts from the fifties. Formerly I hadn't had much more to counter them with than my own curiosity about life, about myself and other people, which actually seemed inconsistent to me. In the meantime it had become possible to conceive of the future not only as a private longing, but as a social perspective. The liberating acquaintance with Marxist philosophy, and the conviction that the people's misery and the deadly intentions of those in power had a capitalist logic to them and were not sheer meaninglessness, routed our life-famished fatalism.

The view of life as a journey toward the perfect moment, as a search for some happiness – however intermittent and arbitrary – was now seen as a devastating error and attributed to withheld information about the real relationships of society and history, to false consciousness and distorted mediation. Christianity, bourgeois science, belief, and disbelief had all been dead ends, leading to places from which nothing could be seen clearly. Before, strategies of survival had consisted in forcing from an unchanging world something more than deficiency, a tiny and elusive piece of happiness. Now, along with many others, I was greedily and breathlessly acquiring a theory which for the first time did not necessarily banish the possibility of change to the world of mere imagination. Through our own efforts, changes could be brought nearer to realization – changes in reality and not in some kind of muddled beyond, beside, outside, or above. Our minds grasped categories that allowed us to imagine what had been nebulous and misunderstood.

Reason entered into our understanding of life. In the light of order and consistency, progressive development and logic, incomprehensible phenomena became comprehensible. A new foundation of meaning was established. There was a certain direction in which events could be arranged. It made sense to look behind us in order to know where we needed to go. All who were part of it could stride along together; the new understanding oriented us and gave us support. To be sure, suspecting that the right analysis lay in our minds and in our legs brought with it many fears: fear of deviating, fear of failure and of futility, fear of not taking part in the changes that are historically possible, or not doing so in the right place and with the right means – for now there was a right and a wrong. Fear about taking the right actions, fear of losing perspective, of not grasping the entire picture, of being ineffectual; fear of falling out with the persons who wanted these same things – for we now had a common task. We felt like human beings who were approaching a new age and were helping to bring it into being. It was as if we were *living* the radical transition to a juster age.

But this was so only in our consciousness; in reality it was a delusion. The theory was borrowed from a century ago and was adopted with many misconceptions. The great change did not take place, either with us or without us. The hopes and the concepts did not correspond to the social facts of our time, to our own history, to our reality. And so there was revolution in the air, but no revolution.

When all images of humanity, all theories about the progressive ennobling of our evil nature begin to sound vaguely comic, when even the noble, natural origins of the victims of civilization prove to be fairy tales; when the revolutionary class does not behave in any recognizably revolutionary way; when experience, once we take a close look, belies all the grand words – there is still and always utopia. The right way, the good way, simply hasn't come into being yet; has never existed, except in human wishes and dreams, except in the vision of a goal. But this goal points unwaveringly in the direction of what doesn't yet exist. When this thing we can imagine did not and does not exist, and when we continuously feel the deficiency of what does exist, then we are projecting ourselves out of the present toward what we are not yet. "It is a matter of learning to hope."[4] I had never unlearned it.

For a few years I had wrestled with the specious discovery of male intellectuals that our sensory experience as nonproletarians led us not toward but away from social reality. We were supposed to perform the psychic and intellectual acrobatics of thinking and acting from the standpoint of the proletariat. But this didn't work: a "proletarian praxis," the only thing that promised to free us from our cognitive limitations, was not our praxis and could not become ours for all our well-intentioned efforts. Marxist epistemology gave women no way to understand their social and personal experience. Our false understanding of the conditions for "correct" knowledge prevented us from seeing reality in our own scandalous and shameful experiences; we turned them instead into trifles or self-deception. Instead of defining ourselves as women we defined ourselves as alliance-seeking petty bourgeois, members of a "broken-class." Our real suffering was warped into the self-pitying complaints of intellectuals who indulge in self-criticism and constantly set themselves apart as members of a "neither/nor" class.

That women experience another reality than men, that women have been controlled by men for over a thousand years, that women have contributed, directly and officially, little or nothing to the culture which determines their lives and yet remain indispensable participants in it – these simple insights justified hopes in the women's movement, hopes which I thought could never be muddled. These insights explained the mistakes and failures of the left as well as the previously incomprehensible discomfort at being placed still and yet again at a remove from reality. They explained doubts and scruples, pains and headaches. They led to changes in living arrangements and changes of address. Never had a decision to turn one's thinking and one's life upside down been so inexorable. My convictions and my emotions brought me to the same place.

The things we each had to do could scarcely be fit into the space of those days and nights. But because it was right, we had a lot of strength. We rallied all our forces. We got in the habit of pushing aside anything that threatened to detour us on our daily paths to our goals, both near and far. We pruned away old contacts, interests, pleasures, and thoughts. What remained had to be clean and sturdy.

The strain, and the many petty disputes and larger rifts among women did not make life exactly easy; but there were explanations for these things which appeased. Besides, we had no choice: there was no going back. We believed in our historical moment, in the destruction and self-destruction of patriarchy. There was no lack of big words about the future. To recite them would make them sound ridiculous. But they were not ridiculous.

It was in 1979, at the time of the NATO resolution, that I began to involve myself with men's actions again. The more I informed myself about the condition of the earth and about the condition of the lords of the apocalypse, the clearer it became what an ineradicable, inescapable legacy would fall to those who want to take on the future, should there be one. For "future" no longer means a transfer of power and a new beginning. What has been done here cannot be undone or unlearned. The dreams of dismantling patriarchy are drawing to an end. The dreams of the future remain as a few broken, if durable, anthropological relics in our cultivated Western heads. They are still apt to be confused with "vital instincts."

Does this mean that feminist hopes have also died? That we're through with them all, all the extravagant, ingenious, hopeful, well-meaning, charitable ideas about how we're more and better than our own reality would indicate?

I don't know. In any case, all the ropes are unraveling. And what is certain is that the ropes *had* to fray, for to live without a rope is the only way that can still be reconciled with self-respect. To live without a rope means to see that men *and* women have unmasked themselves, exposed themselves as creatures from whom there is little to be expected beyond what they have already committed – or omitted, as the case may be. Men have in the course of history permitted all manner of vulgarity, small-mindedness, and negligence;

these have in effect triumphed. They have exposed themselves in all their contempt for themselves and humanity. And women have either done the same thing in their own way or they have simply taken care of these men, tolerated them, put up with them, or ignored them. If anyone did protest, it was mostly alone; and those who protested publicly were also, for the most part, playing solo roles. All the same, I think, we still have some reserves.

My present abstinence in the face of the future is not the result of horror at the unknown or fear that I might have to give up something I've just gotten hold of and want to hold onto. My inability to perceive the future is not due to the dullness of my senses, or to a mental block. Nor does it come from my having ever seen the status quo as a matter of course and therefore not worth changing. It is not to be equated with the astute analysis of Joachim Schumacher, produced in exile during German fascist rule in the thirties, exposing the widespread fear of decline of that time as a class problem: namely, as the fear of the bourgeoisie in capitalist societies, who confused their own impending doom with general decline, with total chaos and the end – a politically perverted Last Judgment.[5]

The future of society has in fact – and not simply in the momentary despair of those whose hopes have been dashed – become void of prospect and change. All *Sturm-und-Drang*-like thinking, openness to what is still to come, desire for transformation, is today subject to ridicule. We can read about the "inspiring, consoling understanding of the world" (Bloch) in the realm of thought and ideas, expressed by humanists of the past, but we won't encounter it or we won't be able to produce it in our own lives. We won't be able to manage, to reconstruct, or to catch up with the facts – except in our heads – and we will remain homeless. These facts have already happened, yesterday, today, tomorrow, the day after tomorrow. So we live in a sealed world, equipped with a kind of thinking and feeling that can't adjust to a static way of life and to this preordained, already ruined world.

What remains, beyond bitter truth, false hopes, the advance of madness and the paralysis of reason?

What is amazing is that, despite all our knowledge of social hopelessness, what remains is not the cynical and diseased view of things, not ugly, hateful bitterness, not only exhaustion and spiritual senility.

What remains is the present.

There is, of course, nothing remarkable about this, for all humans have ever had is their present time. But this present, instead of swinging back and forth between the chronically unbearable and the acutely painful, or withdrawing to deceptive paradises or other refuges, regains its intensity when, with increasing firmness, we refuse to integrate ourselves into the prevailing system of delusion.

We were in the habit of thinking that existence is "infinitely more than it would be if one restricted it to one's present alone."[6] This has become so self-evident that we can scarcely imagine the reverse: that the enriching of the present with material from our imagined, longed-for, hoped-for future actually *impoverishes* the present.

When we look clearly at the content of our days, we see too much that is missed, too much dull, stupid dreaming, and too little of the present. We ignore, overlook, pass over, many moments. And so we miss them. They become unlived life, empty, wasted, spoiled, and lost. But it is not only these moments that are lost: above all we ourselves are lost, as long as we go on evolving into this wretched feeble-mindedness in which all that can be perceived is what's rotten, deceptive, broken-down, out-of-whack, botched-up, unreasonable. Life – one long dirty trick.

Perhaps we should try, at least provisionally, to see the great men in power – who, like their forefathers, still go by the twisted formula "If you want peace, arm for war" – not as giants but as cripples: limited beings into whose laps the means of total destruction have fallen like any other technical innovation, and who unfortunately can liquidate our biological life. What they do not possess is the ideological power to deprive us of life and of personhood, as long as we are alive. Moreover, we ought not to allow our petty rulers, male and female, who time and again all but succeed in killing off our zest for life, to have this effect on us. If we do, we grant them powers of devitalization with which they can turn us into self-tormenting hypochondriacs, into half-corpses who know only how to suffer, or into rigid, frozen people who are no longer able to ward off the forces of self-destruction in ourselves and others. Instead we might implacably *separate* ourselves from everything which restricts our ability to live.

In this way something remains which is not self-delusion, fantasy, projection, or mere consolation. I'm not thinking of anything big: when I truly recognize that things and people are nothing beyond what they are, my gaze becomes more loving instead of more barren.

What I'm thinking of can sometimes be just the sight of some totally insignificant thing that recalls the joy of mere existence, or a feeling in which for one second the beauty of a moment, of a possibility, bursts open in us. What we perceive here is real and present: we can perceive it – not just hope, dream, await, strive for it. We can also encounter it again. Certain moral abstractions, like "goodness," "help," "sympathy," "knowledge," are not just projections of what is missing from us and has thus been transferred to a higher power – or to secularized gods – to make good our own painful deficiencies. Rather, these "values" also arise from the stuff of our own experience with ourselves and others. They can actually be met with from time to time. Nor do they originate solely from the force of a self-righteous moral imperative.

But I also have "big things" in mind. The experience of perfection in music, for example, is no illusion.[7] The "joy" that music can bring, or which it intimates, is no deception. And yet music is not broadcast from the hereafter. It is a human product, completely this-worldly, and its experience is present and humanly possible.

True, such experiences are not merely happy. Like all intense experiences they are also always experiences of endless grief. They offer not the sentimentality of lost and irretrievable happiness or unattainable future happiness, but rather happiness which conveys itself as nonlivable, untranslatable. It remains "unbearable" as an experience; it surpasses us, so to speak, blasts us wide open and destroys itself in the process. Grief and knowledge belong together. We feel both joy and sorrow at the experience of perfection because in it is realized the one aspect of "man" which know we cannot inhabit, at any rate not exclusively and not over time. But the good and perfect experience really happened; it was not just a fleeting apparition. Rather it confronted us with our possibilities, which, although we grasp them far too seldom, we are capable of grasping.

Such thoughts could give me the reputation of a political escapist. Admittedly they do not lead to remedies. Still, I consider such jealous reproaches narrow-minded and stingy. They betray the insistent habit of thinking that the future goal we attach to an action or a thought is the only motive force of life – the habit of seeing the supposed purpose of the action as the cause of the action, as the effective power of future action. And so the stubborn view persists that as soon as we cease to believe in words like "progress," "future," "process," "goal," "development," and so on, the motor of resistance against the destruction surrounding us will come to a standstill.

We need to transgress boundaries. But not in the sense of projecting ourselves out of the present toward what we are not yet, or what this society is not yet. To those male utopias of "eternal peace," of the "classless society," products of their respective historical presents, let us not add female ones. The journeys to utopia, to the contemplation of water stains on the ceilings of apartments and cells, are comfortable, cheap, and soothing.[8] But they are still self-deception.

They are not the transgressions we need. If we want to remain fully alive and fully rational, then let it be for this reason alone: that we have not yet lived our *present* and real possibilities. We are still much less than what we already are.

2

IN ABHORRENCE
OF PARADISE

I am *not* operating from the assumption that we are "in crisis." Those who do are saying "The situation is serious at the moment, but it will get better" – "A crisis has to be gotten through. You hit a low, then it's uphill again." To say "crisis" is to say that everything was once better and will be better again; that development (of security, progress, understanding, economic growth, and so on) just works that way: rise and fall. Sun follows rain and rain follows sun; in the end, though, dawn always breaks.

This is a lot of dumb, distracting blather. The word "crisis" trivializes and obscures. The condition of the earth and of human beings – culminating in the absurdity of nuclear death for every single living creature – and the moral condition of human beings, who have created and tolerated this fact, is not at all well characterized by the term "crisis." We are neither in a crisis nor yet in hell.

The present has been continuously prepared for by a thousand-year development of the dominance of men over women, of rich over poor, of free persons over dependent ones, of so-called civilized peoples over so-called uncivilized. And in this century there have been rehearsals for this present that scarcely any human imagination dared to conceive. The annihilation factor has multiplied by a thousand. What we are now experiencing is no sudden misfortune, but the consequence of a prehistory in which human beings, men and women, were obviously not able to comprehend the crimes of their historical present and in which they "could not distinguish clearly between good and bad."[1]

Our present condition is not the return of a condition which in principle has always existed at certain times, to be replaced by the next condition which has already existed; it is not something which has already happened many times, which existed yesterday and will exist the day after tomorrow. On the contrary, facts, manufactured ones, make this present unique and unprecedented in history. For the patriarchal lust for omnipotence has left the phase of mere hope and preparation and entered the phase of realization. The perfected machinery of annihilation is in fact present on the earth; knowledge about its production is stored in the human brain, is possessed by it, with or without disarmament, with or without deployment, with or without security measures; and a political logic which is the symptom of severe mental sickness and brain poisoning, of collective idiocy and moral deformation, has triumphed. All this makes for the uniqueness of our time.

It is also unique because we have scarcely ever been presented with such an undoctored, crystal-clear view of the results of civilized patriarchal domination. Today everyone can see the full extent of the past and present atrocities on this earth. No one can any longer claim she or he didn't know anything – which was still occasionally plausible during and after the annihilation excesses of the Second World War. The situation is clear. And the tone of annunciation is gone.

Everything has really been said already. Verbal currency is devalued, used up. Language is inadequate. Words are mere worn-out husks that compliantly contain the most various of contents. Everyone speaks of peace; no one knows what peace is. We know at best a poisoned peace. No one has lived on an earth without weapons, without war and the threat of war on a large and small scale. My generation, born in the midst of National Socialism, possibly to National Socialist fathers or even mothers, is aware of the millions of humans slaughtered in the world wars, in concentration camps, in Hiroshima, Nagasaki, and in the wars of the "Third World," which were energetically supported by so-called civilized nations, and of the deterrence crimes of today which have legally stockpiled the equivalent of sixty tons of TNT for every single person in the NATO countries and those of the Warsaw pact. Even if all this is already known and people don't want to hear about it any more, the discrepancy between these facts and our reactions is enormous. Our responses remain conventional, restrained, and disproportionately polite. Behavior appropriate to the situation can scarcely be imagined, so rote and narrow, so disciplined are the available options.

Under these circumstances, everything we believed in and appealed to is thrown into question. The image of the human being as one who wanders and strays, who stumbles and falls, but in the end is still able to come to a reasonable decision, has now become the stuff of parody. The image of the "good person" has become a caricature. The image of human beings as capable of learning, of drawing conclusions from the mistakes and catastrophes we ourselves bring about, has finally become a joke. The luxury of trust is gone. "Man," even though he's still alive, has a ruined air about him. And if I try to analyze him or think about him, I feel like a premature archaeologist studying zombies and monsters.

Since the Enlightenment, with its renunciation of God, knowing and recognizing reality has served to diminish human anxiety. Curiosity and hunger for knowledge made us hope for a progressive solution to the riddle of existence, and for the effective management – for the better, of course – of states and societies, those life associates whose inner workings remain unknown.

Today every new glimpse of reality, every new understanding of connectedness, all further information which we take in, is accompanied by the fear that further knowledge could mean further knowledge of deterioration.

The monstrous virulence of the facts of our time thus tempts us to flee. Following the traditional models, many are tempted to sympathize with prehistoric or apocalyptic conditions of happiness. The scarcity of truly experienced happiness, or the fact that it is threatened, short-lived, and fragile, steers us toward past or future fantasy lands. Like other frightening and inadequate times, this present creates a fervent need for pampering and relaxation, for sun and gentleness, for a healthy life. Such a sight might relieve the tormenting contempt for humanity that takes my appetite away, and dispel the dreary cold. Kingdom of Heaven, Garden of Eden, Eternal Life, Nirvana, End of the World, Utopia, Walden, Walden Two, Sun Country, God's Country, Golden Age, Happy Isles, Islas Mujeres, Women's Land, Land of Milk and Honey; a life which has death no longer in front of it, but rather behind it.

Such ideas of paradise have always been consoling, their prescription healing, their climate soothing. Human misery has always given the greatest boost to utopians. Overcoming ugly human nature and ending the botched state of affairs – this will happen in the hoped-for future, or at least in some completely other place, or else it happened in the past, to which we'd like to return. Later, when I'm grown, later, when I'm old, later, when I'm dead; earlier, when I was small, earlier, before the Fall, before class society, before male domination, before there was any overkill. Real life is transported out of the present, for the present simply does not fulfill our wishes. And so western people's perpetual hopes for the future create a constitution which says it can't live "without hope for better times." This hope for a better life or a better end holds us to the mark, helps somehow to bridge the contradictions, allows us to endure, even when the present is hard to take, makes us patient, blurs our vision, and finally makes us ready to escape from the present at any time. Leaps into the irrational are calming; they fill voids and compensate for deficiencies.

But these paradises are ghostly projects. Their fantasy life has never become reality. History has confirmed none of the hopeful predictions. For two thousand years exploitation of human beings by human beings has been banished in utopias, but these ideal worlds, which exist nowhere, have shown little power to radiate outward, to spill over into reality. The celestial visions, or even those connected with some earthly geography, were not to be accommodated in this world. And so all utopian constructions remained remarkably barren and static. Paradises degenerated again and again into "geometric idylls," peculiarly boring and respectable, marked by sterile harmony and rigidity. *The Peaceable*

Kingdom, for example, painted 150 years ago by Edward Hicks, shows a lion, a tiger, an ape, a lamb, a goat, various kinds of cows, and women playing with children. All together they gaze with large and gentle eyes into a motionless, clean garden of Eden in which all the peacefully sitting or standing figures seem to be rooted to the ground: a paradise.

There is nothing at all to be gained from such contemplative paradisiacal submission, any more than there is from the changeless moment of a falsely conceived "nature." Women know it: this is no paradise. This is stasis, stagnation, an unendurable, constricted non-happiness. Here there is no connection with real people, with their crazinesses, their real and dramatic dreams, with their unpredictability, their outbursts, their occasional laughter.

Evidently it is difficult to imagine paradises in which we really want to live. People can't escape their this-worldly conceptions. And because all the imaginative possibilities and abstractions which are available to us are based on this-worldly experiences, paradises are never really in the beyond, but rather always extrapolations from the here and now. Paradises are laboratories. The characters in them are like automatons, fictions; "not one of them is true, not a one has any more reality than a rag doll. A society of puppets. The inventors are not at all initiated into existence."[2]

We ought to think more about the end of one day than about the end of the world. We should let paradises alone. They are not sanctuaries. We have only one world: this one. We should try to live in our time *hope-lessly* and *in the present.*

Such a sentence not only assaults the love of illusions, but obviously also touches a central nerve, especially for women. The renunciation of the principle of hope is nonetheless unavoidable and unpostponable. I shall clarify what I mean by way of a venerable example, one which until now has never been thrown into question.

Ernst Bloch, the great philosopher of hope, the atheist whose thinking was steeped in the western Christian tradition, the greatly revered comforter and bringer of cheer, left behind a message that was said to be "an oasis in the desert," a source of strength in hard times: we should learn to hope.[3] This alone is the path to human liberation. A massive, universal achievement, the product of a long life, in which an undogmatic Marxist pursued the same question and challenge: the paths of hope for a new society, at a time when change is in the air.

To humanize the world in contrast to the "unfortunate existence of animals, murdering in the most horrible manner, stealing each others' booty."[4] The animals! A work inspired by belief in the future, obsessed with the "not-yet," with the imminent, with the unilluminated "utopian arising of the world." Full of admiration, this progressive philosopher traces "man's" perpetual search for a better life, and ennobles this search as expression of the principle of hope.

What does this look like? Bloch sees Columbus, for example, as someone who was looking for a lost paradise. Here he does not mention that such a quest for paradise always initiated male campaigns of conquest and domination. The paradises of western men – and of their wives, mostly sent for later – are their colonies, large and small. Bloch describes them not as the sites of robbery, of oppression, of presumption, of rape and murder, but rather as "geographic

23

utopias," earthly paradises, since heavenly paradise had proved unattainable. The South Sea, India, Africa, or gold and gemstones: according to Bloch, these are expressions of the search for and the anticipation of a utopian final state. Titan-like, man charges out of the misery of the present to mine the potential of the things that lie before him.

A contemporary example of this kind of assault is the sexual tourism to the women of Thailand by millions of average white men, or the flourishing traffic in women from "Third World" countries to the bars and bordellos of western industrial nations, where West German men are among the major purchasers of that raw material known as woman.

What are the everyday images of hope for women, those that testify against standing in place, for the forward reach of dreams? From time to time, Bloch describes the small glory of daydreams in gender-specific ways: the girl wishes to hide under a cupboard, the boy to climb to a treetop; the girl hopes that someone will break in and carry her away, the boy follows the piper to a beautiful foreign country. "Girls work on their first names as they do on their hairdos," to make themselves more "piquant" to men, boys wish they were on warships with electronic weapons – "bourgeois excesses of a juvenile kind."[5] Whether it's sexual cliches or observations, when it comes to his own examples, Bloch doesn't notice a thing.

His language is loaded with metaphors of war and conquest: "frontline consciousness," "on the frontline of the world process," "hope precisely on the frontline," "battle-field," "victory," "defeat," "gunpowder ready for firings," wanting to be lord of land and sea, to be present on every shore, to "draw up a new map of the earth," to strive for the "summit," to be the "first over the finish line." A symphony's instrumental voices "shoot forward," death is linked to the "hunting instinct," and the "rising of the sun" needs to be "speeded up." It was speeded up, and outdone in beauty, by the first explosion of the atom bomb, which was brighter than a thousand suns and, according to the aesthetic taste of many American witnesses, surpassed the most beautiful of natural phenomena.

Language like this is a betrayal. It is not simply the lapse of a Karl May enthusiast. Instead it reflects in an exemplary way the arrogance, the presumption vis-à-vis nature, the overvaluation of self common to men of the west, and their blind faith in their own kind. In such phallic fantasies their own dream life speaks from the heart. To hope and to have, to hope and to assault, to possess, to master, to colonize, to seize, to anticipate, to engage, to hope and to charge.

The obsession with getting a grip on the future, this drive to create the world, has brought man closer not to peaceful or harmless paradises but to extermination and self-extermination, to cognitive violence and to moral cretinism. In their obsession with the future, men's inventions always turn into weapons, and their intelligence, trained on the future and full of hope, concentrates on devising deterrence systems, or on strategies of securing and expanding power, on enemy investigations, spying and secret services, military reconnaissance, propaganda, seducing and brainwashing the people. Nevertheless, says Bloch, their representative, "Hope is always revolutionary."[6] The most valuable human qualities are bound up with the ability to hope and to design the future.

This is *normal* patriarchal thinking, which prides itself

on being forward-looking and forward-striving. This normalcy has proven to be murderous; clearly what was hoped for was always the wrong thing.

So "normal" women have also become experts in hope – an expertise of a different kind, though. To care for, take care of, nurture, hold together, save, save up, limit, cut back, give, distribute, hold back, always in the right amount, so that everything keeps going, stays in order, or comes to order; so that the misery of one's own existence, the daily tightening of the belt, does not exceed the threshold of what is tolerable. It must be regulated by keeping your eye tirelessly on tomorrow and the day after in your own little world, on dreams of a better life or, mostly, of love. And when conflicts arise, hoping that everything will get straightened out, that the situation will right itself or can be righted, hoping that things can't really be all that bad. Women's system of order is their system of hope. Their sympathizing, empathizing, thinking ahead, accompanying, limiting, figuring, directing, producing, understanding, disapproving, controlling, judging, prejudging, is all in the interest of producing, out of a small and easily disrupted collection of people in a little corner of the world – the "relationship," the family, the affinity group, the scene – a stable unity, hopefully safe for the future, a unity which no one is allowed to break away from. A permanent exertion and straining of thoughts toward whatever it is these others, the "near and dear ones," can be seen to be doing, and will do; a ceaseless straining of antennae toward the signals they broadcast; a reception of distress signals even before they are sent, and then anticipatory intervening, engaging, entering presciently into shifting alliances with those involved – in order to salvage, provisionally, a superficial harmony.

And all on the basis of a wide-eyed trust in everything that happens outside our own field of vision, a perfect defense mechanism of female morality. Or else on the basis of a markedly concealed disgust – the flip side of this trust – which likewise evades reality, which does not look, does not touch, and keeps whatever offends at arm's length so that it cannot affect the unfolding of one's own wishes.

Women are often outstandingly well qualified to establish this medium of a delicate balance based on hope, of a peace never free of poison. This has been psycho-hygienically demonstrated. It is the reason for women's social indispensability. Many claim to thrive in such an atmosphere, and entering it brings on a mild sense of well-being. Establishing the helpful climate of hope for the good and peaceful trust requires the capacity for tuning out, for a warm blindness. This capacity protects against breakups, breakdowns, break-ins; against partings, which women are not very good at. It is medicine, relief from pain. Renouncing the gentle luxury of trust leads first into cold and unknown realms. Seeing is often unpleasant. It disturbs the ambience, the calm; it disturbs good form. It destroys the mood. Mistrust, ready to break out at any time, makes life disorderly.

Why exactly should we hold fast to a psychological disposition – namely, hope – which, rather than transcending the moral level of this culture, can only fix it in place? Why do we need hope for the future when we refuse to accept our present existence? Why should the tension in which we exist and out of which we act stem from future hopes? We can expect from hope no solid reason not to harden, not to shrink or grow weary in this time. Why should our experience that longing almost always surpasses fulfillment justify our stubbornly clinging to the idea that "it's all going to get better"? Why, today of all times, should this very clinging to a stale and discredited construct make up what is human about human beings? This world does not justify such a thing. There must be some other place to go with our unfulfilled wishes, with the disparity between conception and reality. And even if there were a reason to hope, it would have nothing to do with us, so to speak, for we are incapable of recognizing it.

Whenever hope and illusion become the source of the will to live, all knowledge of reality becomes highly threatening, since at any time a new piece of information might remove the grounds for this hope. This is exactly the case now. When life is motivated by hope for improvement, denial of reality is necessarily renewed and fortified. We would have to become or remain illusionists, to return to female infantilism, to dumb goodwill, to faith, to hopeless female naivete. And in this way we would finally do ourselves in.

We should learn to live in the *present*. Our situation forces us to recognize that we cannot postpone and defer our demands of ourselves and of others. We cannot afford to transfer all that we can do and be to the future. *The test is right now.* Everything that we have to do, we have to do now.

I am, then, pleading for this completely rotten present. It is our only opportunity. It is the only life that we have. It and it alone contains the means to develop our powers.

To concentrate on the present, to dethrone interpretations and to renounce the pressure of the future is not at all an act of despair or a symptom of fatigue, weakness, and resignation; rather it is a liberation from filth, a kind of cleansing.

Nor does concentrating on the present mean a restriction of spiritual elbow room, as if we were balancing on a slowly moving point, a tiny instant of time, and before and behind this point were nothing but darkness, emptiness, and question marks. The abstract conception that the present is "nothing," because every single moment can be divided into what's just past and what's about to come, contradicts the experience of being living creatures who can influence what they produce, what they have produced or will produce, and what they perceive. The present is that stretch of time which has not yet retreated from our influence, in which we have possibilities. For instance, when a child is building a toy city on the floor, all past moments from the beginning of construction belong to the present, just as do all ideas of how to continue building. What started to go up three hours ago can at any time be rebuilt, changed, or dismantled. Now the track for the locomotive. It gets smoke sticks in the chimney. Oh no, the track has to go by the houses because the smoke smells so good. Now we need trees. I'll have to find some in the box. . . . Everything is constantly being corrected, expanded, made use of. It can take a long time.

The whole process of making something and interacting with what one has made remains in the present as long as it contains something changeable and useful. If an adult were to come and forbid the child to build any further, order her to pack up her things, or take them away, then from that moment on the game would be over, the city destroyed – that is, the past would have begun.

Past, present, and future are therefore not really concepts for ordering time. Rather, they order my *possibilities,* my productivity. The present is that period of time in which events are still flowing and are not yet or no longer closed to us or taken out of our hands. What we can still take back is still around, is not yet destroyed.

The present, then, is not the unchanging, concrete moment, the stationary period of time, the frozen possibility, apathy, inaction. Nor does the present consist simply in the visible, measurable, quantifiable elements of material fact. Dreaming, for example – in contrast to the constructed utopia, to fantasy and illusion and institutionalized paradises – is a phenomenon of the present. It takes place here, yet is not bound to the momentary point in time, for it reaches backward and forward and mingles tenses with its own surprising logic. It dissolves space and time, but it unfolds *now;* it is not a test run or a rehearsal for the future. It exploits the possibility of thinking, sensing, and expressing in the present while embracing all time, something that is scarcely possible in waking life. It joins together seemingly unconnected events and times. We can, in the present, experience more than our eyes can tell us. Dreams can open our eyes to new possibilities in waking life. But we have learned to disregard their teachings and restrict their field of influence, because the information they yield can be threatening to orderly normal life and thought. For dreams know too much.

The present has to do with *clarity.* The German language conveys this in expressions such as: I make something present to myself, something is present to me, I am present to myself. This means I am present with all my senses and faculties, concentrated on something, whatever it happens to be. I summon the past, experiences, and desires, and bring them all to one point.

I operate from the assumption that in this rotten present we have the possibility of living and learning to live; that our sole salvation lies in being completely oriented to this life, as intensely as possible, in exhausting the givens and seizing

hold of life. What interests me is whether I can live irrevocably without hope, whether rebellion is possible without
hope.

Such formulations lead to great misunderstandings.
Many people associate the word "life" with something like
leisure time and vacation, or think of personal relationships.
Life is confused with private life and intensity with love. The
call to life is heard as the plea for an individualistic retreat
into a private life focused on relationships and culture, as if,
with a resigned shrug of the shoulders, you could from now
on give yourself over sensuously to "enjoying life" – but what
life? This is not what I mean. Reducing life to private life and
intensity to love relationships (mostly understood as sexual
relationships) I see as an all too female narrowing of emotional
and intellectual possibilities to the one realm in which women
have traditionally sought to pursue their life desires and, if
they weren't fulfilled, to further pursue them, only with
different persons. This is unacceptable.

Evidently many people miss the seemingly clear word
"resistance." I can no longer use it without prejudice. It is
static and reactive. In any case, we have to come up with a
new concept for what we called resistance. Resistance cannot
be something that is quantifiable and identifiable by certain
organized actions; it is a growing equation of our entire
person, our entire lifetime, with deviation from the norms
that define this society. As a result, it is no longer possible
to speak of life on the one hand and resistance on the other
– to divide and re-add life and resistance, to split up life and
action, action and relaxation, thinking and speaking. Life is
resistance and resistance is life. Everything else is a sham.

From this perspective, one which does not trust goal-
oriented strategic thinking, it is not particularly important

whether a political action is successful or promising. For I see it as at least questionable whether we with our interventions, our actions and ideas, can prevent further arming, deployment, or war, further burial of Europe or of the earth. Under existing conditions what we fear can come true – and much has come true – regardless of whether or not individual human beings have remained inhuman and lifeless. An action is "right," then, if it brings to expression, puts into the world, those moral, intellectual, and emotional forces which deviate from the violent patriarchal structures. This is what is decisive, whether or not this world can still be changed by it.

It is not just a matter of physical survival. If humanity is actually as rotten, dull, and malicious as it may well turn out to be, then it should go under. It deserves no other end – it deserves the death which it has prepared for itself. It does not deserve to have this life, to populate this earth, to realize its own possibilities for good. And the bomb must be the symbol of its own essence: power, destruction, contempt, and boundless stupidity.

I do not love this merely biological existence enough to see the possible human-made finale as the greatest catastrophe. I see as even greater the catastrophe of wasting, in the time remaining to us, our possibilities as women with *this* history and in *this* present, of throwing them away, of sleeping through them; that is, of falling behind ourselves.

To expand our possibilities: this alone might be some kind of fulfillment. Western people have for the most part put off fulfillment and deliverance from bondage; they have too seldom been in the position to find both in themselves, to direct nostalgia and expectation toward themselves. Such fulfillment must not remain an empty formula that can materialize only in some future world – and then, of course, only thanks to a supernatural power existing above or beyond us – without our ever having ourselves known what it might actually mean to live in fulfillment and deliverance.

The Christian West has historically backed away from the claim of its religious founder that the Kingdom of God was neither above nor below, but within us. The very quest for this Kingdom of God itself contradicted the desire for great, manly, forward-marching steps. And so it seemed more opportune to transfer this kingdom to the future. This way all the manufactured scandals of the present could be justified. And the God in human beings could not be found.

I am not a Christian. In fact I have sympathized mostly with the immoralists, with those beyond good and evil. They were always the radicals who located themselves outside conventions and tried to think without models, without parallels and predecessors. They did this in times when those in power claimed to be moral. But the situation has gradually reversed. The intellectual and cultural tradition of the Christian West, in all its contradictoriness, brutality, and yet unbelievable richness, shows that morality is not just a straitjacket tailored by whoever happens to be in power and worn by whoever happens to be unfree.

Morality, the evaluation of human beings and their deeds, is above all a human opportunity which we as women can either lose all over again or else can perceive anew, without models to follow. To speak of morality is not fashionable, not at all à la mode. In post-Enlightenment thought, in leftist and feminist thinking, "morality" has scarcely had a place; it is somehow an embarrassing word. There is no conceptual or linguistic convention for this aspect of humanity, especially not for women. We grope for words, speak in babytalk about "good" and "bad." The words are simplifications, or they are preachy, bigoted, accompanied by a pointing of the pedagogical finger.

Every woman and man can grasp the fact that humans should act like human beings because they are able to do so. If they had to be good only as long as there was a God, all humanity would collapse the moment he was no longer believed in. But history has not proved that the capacity for moral judgment is dependent on belief in God; belief in God could be lost and superseded by other beliefs. "God is dead" does not mean that everything is allowed, that no one is watching. Morality is not tied to divine bookkeeping. God and humanity are not business partners checking out each other's claims. It is this kind of business thinking that has led to the faltering of discipline and reliability as soon as there is no dear God in heaven observing and rewarding us.

Besides, generations of self-satisfied Christian deeds still appeal to this concept – generations of persecutions, tortures, burnings at the stake, military campaigns; libraries full of intellectual theological exegeses that justify injustice; Sunday services and Masses full of shady doings, distracted efforts at prayer, half-hearted confessions, and pious peace-making.

Morality, demanded and laid out in the terms of those in power, meant the repeated enforcement of conformity and integration, the tranquilizing and exploitation of individual subjects. This understanding of morality calls on individuals to cause no evil. The individual is occupied his whole life long, remorsefully or in gentle self-righteousness, with displaying a clean slate on his own doorstep. He tries, through his moral rules, to restrain himself as much as possible. This is practical and saves work for church and state. So the moral ideals of the Christian West were for the most part, practically speaking, in no way revolutionary.

When Nietzsche railed against the Christian moral system it was because it adapted and reduced human beings to hypocritical moral cowardice and led to hypocrisy or despair. The symbolic God of Christianity, the Lord, the Ruler, the Almighty, the All-Powerful, is the epitome of the male quest for power. Faced with this God, an individual essentially has two possibilities: to envy Him, even to be a bit like him, great and powerful; or to knuckle under, to be very small and inconspicuous. Women's evil deed, their "sin," is more often the latter, and women need a completely different definition of "sin" than men.

When human morality is no longer obeyed within the framework of individual horse-trading with God, with whom everyone secretly wants to make a deal and be rewarded for good behavior, it begins to be explosive – that is, when it has become a collectively acquired and collectively displayed quality of human beings, one which is in contradiction to what the authorities think is right.

The ethical kernel of the New Testament, the Sermon on the Mount, requires of people that they give up property and security, violence and retaliation. In the Christian churches, these commandments were seen as meaningful counsel for living, but undesirable and unfulfillable from a political point of view. This fundamental infeasibility of the commandment of nonviolence became the basis for its historical ineffectiveness; Christians murdered, massacred, and fought "righteous wars" with the Sermon on the Mount in their packs. The experience of nonviolent uprisings, especially in India and North America, and the positions of pacifists during the two world wars and in the current antiwar and peace movement, have impressed the contents of the Sermon on the Mount even more strongly upon the consciousness of Christians and non-Christians alike. This Sermon is a radical political affair. It surpasses the usual humanitarian arrangements of nations. After two thousand years it corrects the Pharisees' prevailing understanding of the law. It outbids all lawfully established rules of human social life. It makes its claims universally, for all people. For here it is demanded, written in stone and without any qualification, that we make peace with our enemy, with every enemy, and refrain from any retaliation.

The question is whether this can be women's morality as well. The commandment to be peacemakers, understood in the political sense, was and is addressed to men. For men and for the rulers of the earth it is revolutionary now, just as it was then. The version of peacemaking that women have practiced is something else; peacemaking with limited vision serves the rulers' warmaking. We cannot simply rediscover a submerged and ignored teaching, not even one which a man named Jesus, who more or less deviated from the patriarchal majority, recognized as lifesaving for the members of his own sex. Even two thousand years ago it was not conceived with women in mind. Apparently it was not socially necessary to find an equivalent for women, who were less conspicuous; because of their complementary and subservient living arrangements with men they were automatically included. But morality is not an absolute law of behavior.

We must rethink everything. We have fallen behind. For at the moment we know what it is *not* more than what it is. The only thing to do at this moment is to proceed antisystematically and aphoristically, or lyrically, or musically.

. . . What we have are commentaries, notes, broken-off arguments, suggestions. But these are not arbitrary.

A few weeks ago I saw a documentary film about Ravens-brück, the concentration camp for women. The director, a Polish Jew who had survived the camps, said in her commentary at the screening that she did not know whether the next generation (ours, that is) was to be found guilty or exonerated. As became clear in the discussion that followed, some people were surprised, alienated, or enraged by this remark. They had had nothing to do with it, their parents didn't know anything about it, they weren't even born yet. The former inmate remained stubbornly silent at these protestations.

I think our complicity exposes itself in the extent to which we fail to grasp the present. To the present belongs knowledge about the past. The distancing shudder – "How could such a thing ever happen?" – is a lie.

A young woman said in the discussion, "We can't really feel today what happened then because it doesn't affect us directly, immediately. We lack the experience. We can't suffer either, but one must suffer in order to become involved. All present dangers are merely potential, not real. . . ." The constant talk of being "directly affected" justifies an indulgent narrowing of feelings and imaginative powers. We can think and feel about far more than what happens to take place in our own lives, however troubled or untroubled they are. How can you say "I can't feel that"? Isn't it cause enough that this earth is being systematically prepared for its destruction before our very eyes? What else needs to happen? If you think you can't "suffer," what kind of sick are you?

Hanna Levy-Hass, a survivor of the Bergen-Belsen concentration camp, writes, "I will measure every person as to what he was and would have been in our situation by the criterion of present reality. In order to form an opinion about someone, to value or not to value her, to love or not to love: in the end it will all depend on what her attitude, her psychic, physical, and moral reaction was or has been in these bleak years of great trials. . . . I will never again be able to separate the world of my thoughts and my reflections from the events of the war. . . . To forget is to fail."[7] This goes for the present time as well.

3

FROM DECEPTION
TO UN-DECEPTION:
ON THE COMPLICITY
OF WOMEN

Since Europe's first utter nihilist and most famous God-killer Friedrich Nietzsche spoke over a hundred years ago, various clever and malicious analyses of the finale of Western culture have emerged. Under the weight of the devastations of both of the world wars of this century, in an "age full of nihilistic fever" (Camus), the collapse of this civilization has been ever more dramatically laid bare. The authors of the decline naturally spoke of humans, of humanity being at an end, not of men.[1] We feminists later took reassuring note of this. We said: those are not our insights. If the patriarchy takes its wretched leave, then only from the limited perspective of men – whether existentialists, nihilists, moralists, or pessimists – is it always identical to the ultimate end of world history. Men can only think of destroying themselves – and bringing everything down along with them. This was just one of a thousand good reasons for women to separate from the male point of view. Here, as everywhere, we had been subsumed. Here, fortunately, they didn't mean us. If men recognize their own downfall, we said, they are incapable of imagining the simultaneous rise of women.

In the meantime the civilized societies of the white man have managed so thoroughly to destroy living conditions on the earth that it's become an absolutely insane challenge just to want – or be able – to live at all, to develop our living senses, to preserve them and use them and tirelessly fight their atrophy. In fact we have no certain future toward which our curiosity and our rebellion can be directed. Instead we have a unique, brief or endless but nonetheless irrevocable present, whose ironclad continuation is linked to the work of nuclear and conventional mass murderers.

The force driving the following reflections is not the mournful verification of these monstrous truisms; nor is it the question of those social and individual energies which the patriarchal powers and puppets harness to their deeds of destruction. Rather it is the question of how women, who for the most part did not participate in the production of knowledge about the means of destruction, or in their political implementation, are involved in this process.

The conviction of women's *complicity* in those developments which have as their end the eventual and unheroic liquidation of humanity leads to a compelling conclusion, and to come to it is life-threatening. It confronts us with our own end and not with our new beginning.

The fact that men in power have achieved the possibility of manifold and total annihilation sends us into a fatally delayed tailspin. Women have failed. We cannot relieve ourselves of the consequence which an acknowledgment of this failure must bring: namely, the risk of total uncertainty. All self-evident truths have come to an end, along with all reliable categories of understanding. We must go beyond the conventions which held our feminist thought and conscience in place. Our perceptions must have been seriously flawed. With the questions that arise, we cannot cling to our current systems of meaning, hopes, and illusions, to our way of seeing and our way of living of the last ten years and all the years before that – not even if the consequence is confusion. For it is possible that all new thoughts initially produce more confusion than light; and perhaps it really is just a matter of seeing clearly, of becoming more keenly aware, and of no longer hoping.

"In this society there is always war. Not war and peace. There is only war."[2] To point to our daily war remains inadequate. Harassment, abuse, discrimination, underpayment, sexism everywhere we look is our everyday experience or observation; conflict is the stable, continuous, everyday condition of women and it masters us or we master it with more or less success. These war scenes are, it is true, governed by the same laws as the production of weapons, poison gases, surveillance systems, of lying and stupefying ideologies: all are governed by the logic of power and domination. Nonetheless, we cannot ignore the difference between our countless daily wars and the worldwide escalation of nuclear, chemical, and biological means of annihilation.

If women cling to the belief that the ruling powers have always flaunted their might and that our present is thus fundamentally no different from all others in which men have threatened and ruled and destroyed – "Why are we getting so upset? The situation is nothing unusual!" – then we're fooling ourselves.

The confusion lies in an inadmissible abstraction which

many women seize upon with a great sense of discovery and relief: that the history of patriarchy has always been marked by continuous destruction, whose aim has been not so much destruction itself as the show of omnipotence and superior strength. In this elegant abstraction the uniqueness of our present, which already encompasses decades, once again falls victim to repression. That there is more than a slight technological difference between bows and arrows and atomic overkill, between curare and chemical and bacteriological warfare, no one will deny. But the claim that since August 6, 1945, when the United States exploded the atom bomb over Hiroshima (or since July 16, 1945, the first test-bombing in the New Mexico desert), this patriarchy has entered an epoch which no longer admits parallels to any other known epoch encounters stubborn resistance. Thirty and then twenty years ago, when the situation was clearly named, this was the case not only for the "drugged masses" but also for the still heterogeneous peace or antiwar movement – and obviously also for women.[3]

The uniqueness of the "time capsule" in which we find ourselves consists in this: that since the innocent development and forceful expansion of nuclear and "conventional" weapons, of chemical and bacteriological mass-annihilation capabilities, of the technology of electronic warfare through military satellites in space and worldwide listening posts, the patriarchal wish for omnipotence and total control has stepped out of the realm of mere fantasy, fiction, and experiment into the realm of complete realizability.[4] It no longer has to be invented, imagined, dreamed up. It already *is*.

But as well known as these facts are, they have still not completely freed us of womanly hope: it *can't* be that bad! The boring, undramatic, and static nature of our condition

seduces us with such consolations. The invisible and pro-
longed agony of the rapidly approaching radical catastrophe
nourishes them. Waiting engenders bad ideas and fosters
repression. And so new deceptions are created that cloud
reality. For some jokers on the left this reality is already too
hackneyed. With journalistic panache, they have already
outgrown "the wave of apocalypse" and "the chic of despair."
These, they say, have to be traced back to the general "negativity of the human spirit," to the cyclically recurring human
craving for catastrophes and endings, or simply to our current
taste for the tragic.[5] The facts, which have rather quickly
lost their spectacular impact and become commonplace,
nonetheless remain.[6]

The question of the complicity of women in the destruction processes directed by men and in men's destructive
logic meets – at least within the women's movement – with
iron resistance. It provokes rage. "Complicity" is a word that
makes many women recoil. It sounds unfeminist, antifem-
inist, as if a new class of guilty women were being created
and old culprits exonerated.

The complicity of women is first of all a claim about
our present history. It is dishonest to assert that women lead
a life of their own parallel to patriarchal actions and yet fairly
and perhaps increasingly independent of them – in a different
place, so to speak. I believe rather that an amalgamation of
sexually differentiated interests in civilized patriarchies has
produced women's complicity, in order that they will not
betray men, resist them, or hinder their actions. In effect,
this seems to have succeeded – despite all struggles, resis-
tances, and refusals. Instrumental to this success are above
all the norms of sexual complementarity and sexual equality.

We become collaborators whenever we accept an idea

of self-completion that consists of developing and acting out a restrictive "feminine" repertoire complementary to the "masculine" one; whenever women attach themselves to the male as the subordinate opposite sex; whenever women support and protect the male individual by structuring their own spheres – especially those of the home, of "social conscience," and of humanity – in such a way that the man is left free for his actions.

We become collaborators whenever we accept offers of equality – namely, to think and act according to patriarchal logic and to confuse this with human logic; whenever women adapt to the status quo of male achievements and develop fellow feeling with their male comrades, colleagues, or lovers. Women thus become at best men's competitors, but not their partners. They are taken into the male fold; they present no threat. They belong.

Women are implicated in the success of the material and ideological power of patriarchy, and not only as passive victims. If women insist on a quasi-colonial status, it is not only in forced compliance with male interests. As a result of sexual divisions of labor and a certain ideological distance from men, which have been used by men and by women themselves to keep them from male affairs, a woman gains some free space as well as chains – a living space she can count on, a house, apartment, children, a time of the day without her husband, some independence, some self-sufficiency, some competence. But this fragment of a private world – which has contracted sharply with the ideology and the realization of civilized patriarchies, at best restabilizing during wartime, when women organized their own lives and those of their children while men went around killing each other – this privacy never fostered the development of a female counterforce and identity. The special mix of distance and dependency in the relations between the sexes seems always to have served to pacify women, to bind them to hopes as if they were realities, so that the "murderous normalcy" could be taken, even by them, as natural.[7]

The arguments against a "complicity of women" sound plausible at first: complicity is a concept that brings women before the prosecutor's table, or even turns us into each others' prosecutors. It imposes a blame-the-victim mentality without acknowledging women's many attempts, historically and in the present, to resist. It ignores all attempts to live outside the blame-the-victim scenario. It parcels out guilt and puts the burden on women, instead of further accusing those who force women to renounce their own development and resistance to become pillars of support for men – voluntarily or involuntarily enabling men to develop their own destructive powers. The concept of complicity encourages indiscriminate guilt-slinging. In its coarseness, it obscures the countless subtle gradations of women's participation in the catastrophic perversion of life. Instead it simply assumes women went along, as it were collectively, with this eminently stupid and fateful march into disaster; it assumes women were in agreement with these goals or, knowing of them, made their own accustomed handicrafted contributions toward realizing them. It would be more accurate to use differentiating terms like "assistant," "fellow traveler," "accessory," or to speak of "sharing responsibility" and "sharing guilt."

Complicity is, finally, a concept which imposes on us the burden and duty of proof: namely, that we lay out and explain our own actions and responsibilities, our own collaboration. It thus fixates us on the eternal history of female pathology and traps us in a way of thinking that shackles us to our deformities and handicaps instead of wrenching us out of our fettered thoughts and endless complaints, instead of sweeping our minds free. Isn't this question of our complicity something of a perfunctory exercise – as if we were told to inspect our luggage and put it in order before rigorously throwing it overboard? If now, on top of everything else, we have to establish proof of our complicity, aren't we forcing ourselves yet again to deal with our dreary past? Aren't we crippling our ability to imagine utopias for the present and the future? In all these ways the concept has a demoralizing effect on us and in turn paves the way for every kind of antiwoman politics.

These counterarguments rest in part on assumptions which to my mind are no longer valid. The word "complicity" evokes a kind of sisterly impulse to protect those women who seem under attack. I find this protectiveness inappropriate. It's not a question of assigning guilt. The thought of complicity is not to be ranged among the many female self-accusations and self-reproaches which arise in the stagnant air of a repressive bondage of thought and feeling. On the contrary; every step away from our previous understanding demands something of us, leads us to new battlegrounds – full of sorrow, perhaps, but without self-pity.

To speak of female complicity is provocative. The autonomous women's movement gained its initial self-confidence, energy, and creativity from the fact that women absolved themselves of responsibility for the violence they suffered and for the depravity of this society. Our communal rejection of guilt justified the demand for autonomy as a political consequence. In the process, the linking of autonomy with the victim theory became a trap. We cannot base our autonomy on our victim status. We cannot be untainted and autonomous victims. One rules out the other. Humans decide for themselves what they are; this fundamental minimum applies to women as well.

The women's movement is not simply undergoing an ideological crisis for which we unfortunately don't have the right ideas or measures at this moment. Our situation is much more definitive. We seemed in much better shape than the liberals and leftists, who had been stuck in their identity crisis for a long time. The intellectual and economic bankruptcy of liberalism exposed it as hopelessly antiquated. Marxism proved to be a historical theory suitable neither as surrogate religion nor as a timeless course in political behavior. We feminists were in a comparatively good position. We had no theory, but we were in the right: Women all over the world are oppressed and our historical moment has come. Patriarchy has hit rock bottom. Men are finished. The historical redemption of male power is at hand. Women will begin to seize their rights, overthrow their oppression, and win back the territory men have taken from them. Women will lay claim to what men have considered their natural possession for thousands of years. And every war is a step "towards the self-destruction of patriarchy."[8]

Now, however, it appears that the earth itself, which still forms the ground for all social and political transformations and for every new beginning, is on its way to becoming a concentration camp from which there is no escape. It has inherited a terminally ill legacy which would make a hell of all further life on its soil – if there is any. For this legacy is ineradicable, and there is no escape route by which we can renounce it. It makes all human generations to come dependent, powerless, and unfree.

The earth has been overloaded with atomic explosives whose potential for mass murder exposes all living beings to extreme and constant danger. Even disarmament – should it, against all expectations, succeed – could not erase what we know about the production of the means of annihilation. Knowledge about their manufacture and restoration will in the foreseeable future be possessed by around forty countries on the earth, and by who knows how many individual brains.[9] Even a "disarmament of the mind" cannot eradicate this reality.

The earth is occupied by an atomic industry that needs an army of the most reliable workers just to keep nuclear accidents at a minimum. In order to guarantee safety, it requires a surveillance apparatus which can in the long run be produced only by a totalitarian state. One of its main tasks will be monitoring the "abuse" of radioactive substances and preventing theft – from nuclear power plants, from waste recycling plants, or in transport – of fissionable material that could be made into bombs. Eight to ten kilograms of plutonium is enough for a functional bomb the size of the Nagasaki bomb, an insignificant amount relative to the quantity produced every year in West Germany. But even in tiny amounts from two to three grams, plutonium in powder or compressed form is extremely valuable because of its potential for extortion. Safeguarding against accidents from the outside and sabotage from within, against spying and nuclear extortion, involves not only scarcely imaginable protection measures as well as personnel control, but also advancing the security boundary into society itself. This means an expansion of government surveillance and observation procedures into the general population, especially the preventive surveillance of all inhabitants in the vicinity of nuclear technology installations, as well as investigation of the ideological environs of all opponents of nuclear power and warfare who could be considered hostile to the state. In order to achieve sufficent electronic monitoring of the professional, private, and social activities of potential "enemies of the state," a central data bank is needed, with information about private initiatives, environmental groups, troublemakers and deviants of every persuasion, along with the analysis of petitions, telephone and mail monitoring, intelligence agents, hidden microphones, and so on. Add to this the intensification of political criminal law, reduction of the right to demonstrate, increase in the ranks and firepower of police, detectives, and border guards. All these measures can be legitimated by every state as "required by the facts" – such as the prevention of nuclear terrorism in the interest of protecting the general populace.[10]

Beneath the earth's surface are spreading countless toxic waste deposits of unknown liquid residues, into which the industrial countries daily pour their tons of waste from power facilities, industrial concerns, and sewage plants. The extent of these deposits is as much as two million square meters. Also stored in the earth, mostly in secret locations, are chemical and biological weapons and shells filled with nerve gas.[11] In urban areas, the earth has been built up and killed off with concrete, which as of now cannot be disposed of by any chemical or mechanical means and does not dissolve through any natural decomposition process. These developments inevitably determine the lifeforms of all living creatures existing within or between them. A steadily growing portion of the earth's natural productivity is being damaged and destroyed. Through the spread of chemical materials and heavy metals, the release of radioactivity, and the effects of agribusiness, everything the earth provides – air, water, forest, soil – has been diminished or has become dangerous for all living beings.[12] If animals and plants were our "brothers and sisters," then nature, disfigured and plundered, could have no other wish than for human beings, these "anti-lifers," to get out as quickly as possible and hasten their ultimate exit from this earth.[13] But human beings will hardly do this without taking at least a part of nature along with them.

The containment and management of durable products of destruction, the avoidance of contaminated areas, knowledge that information about the annihilation of nature and humans cannot be unlearned, the endlessness of existential uncertainty and inadequate control, fear of nature's hatred and wrath and at the same time the task of restoring this wreck of an earth to an ecologically functioning biosphere – these are the determinants of all further social and political life. They also determine future power relations. All politics is irrevocably situated in an atomic world and all further existence on the earth lives under the permanent threat of its potential liquidation. The "lords of apocalypse" can bring it about themselves, by intention, stupidity, chance, or weariness. In having within their reach the end of any individual region, or of all regions, they have reached the pinnacle of omnipotence – and of criminality. This property of our rulers makes the age in which we are living "the terminal age of humankind," even if it should continue to drag on endlessly in an undramatic decline.[14] For what has been wrought here is not to be undone.

The dreams of the end of patriarchy have dissolved. No one will want to inherit this legacy. The disempowerment of the white man could actually be in his own interest some day – that is, if he himself gets sick of controlling and monitoring the consequences of his presumption and perversion, of proving himself equal to them, of having to dispose of his own deadly garbage. In any case I do not believe that removing men from the earth is an attractive prospect for us. A worse nightmare can hardly be imagined. In spite of all our complicity, we don't deserve this. We cannot save this poisoned planet; it cannot be the mission of women to set about making good again the steady contamination of life. To choose to take on the dirty work, to take charge of the material and psychological rubble, would yield simply another variant on the image of female self-sacrifice and female housework: sweeping up the ruins of patriarchy.

The challenge to live is no longer comparable to other times. The past seems to take on the exotic and irrelevant quality of being on vacation. We can regard it with feelings of sorrow or wonder; we can enjoy its legacies and use it to distract ourselves or to recover from the present and the future. But we can no longer learn from the past what we used to think we could learn. The expectation that our history moves in continuous developments, in systematic steps that follow one another, has been called into question. Our time is unique, unprecedented; it is the time of nuclear patriarchy, the logic and illogic of which completely determines our identity, our struggles, and our perspective – whether or not we want to believe it.

As soon as women work their way out of an ahistorical, episodic consciousness restricted to the present and try to range their existence along a contradictory continuum of the historical development of female power and powerlessness, the path will open up. In any case, to look for sites of identification in the past, to be inspired by strong women and fearless resistance fighters or by female solidarity in a homeland periodically free of men – as in wartime – is simply not enough. The transfer of historical experiences has become more questionable than ever before. The "mystical uniting of past, present, and future" that has become so popular – the simple visualization of mythical or historical female figures, as if they were standing beside us today uttering words of comfort – is unambiguously inappropriate.[15]

At the same time in this seemingly ahistorical situation there arises a boundless nostalgia for a time whose future we might still be able to influence, in which we could still fight the development of the intention to annihilate, instead of having to accommodate somehow to the fact of total capability to annihilate. The longing for a prenuclear time is the longing for a life freed of the moral lead weights that we drag along through this time: namely, having to face the fait accompli that the men of white patriarchy have been able to acquire apocalyptic powers unhindered, allowing the dumbest representatives of their sex to dispose of them; that women have looked on passively; that men have made a mess of the earth and that women either could not stop it, or didn't notice, or trustingly approved, or resourcefully supported it.

All this we can bear with the help of the powerful old lie, the motto of the "German Women's Order," the Red Cross of the National Social Democratic Party, which many women today still carry in their hearts: Faith, Love, and Hope.[16] Faith in human goodness; love for the strong man and his children; hope for victory. Or today's version: faith in our suffering's usefulness to God, the gods, or the stars; love for illusions, fantasies, and dreams; hope in meaning, in the beyond, in the future, in rebirth, in peace – or simply hope that everything will somehow go on, and turn out only half as bad.

Or we can finally begin, singly and simply, to see clearly, to revolt against all systems of meaning and live in our time *proudly* and *hope-lessly*. Granted, this sounds demoralizing; but the point is not to inspire courage. It's not a question of ministering to the soul, of social work, or of any kind of rehabilitation. It is high time we began de-moralizing, dis-illusioning and un-deceiving. Women have successfully accomplished one of the essential historical tasks which civilized patriarchy delegated to them: namely, the upholding of certainties and illusions. Responsible for the transmission of cultural values and cultural lies, women have countered the lax and cowardly tendencies that have always overtaken men and children. With constancy and discipline, women have sustained hope for the better – and thus set an example of faith in the continuation of life through all crises. To all those without courage, women have shown by example that this life is meaningful and in order.

This is not to say that all this came about through mere naivete or short-sighted stupidity. But the priority of harmony in the private sphere seems to have been achieved by a tradeoff. Woman sacrifices what she knows to it – as in the short story "Day X" by Marie-Luise Kashnitz.[17] The woman, who is nameless, knows one morning that the bomb will fall today. The people around her – her husband, her sons, the school principal, the priest, the neighbors – know nothing about it and go merrily about their important business. The woman's tentative attempts to orient herself, which rush her through the day, signal to her that her nerves are shot. No one takes her seriously. Her knowledge becomes increasingly inscrutable. She expresses it only through hints; the moment her suggestion is rejected, she withdraws and concedes to the others. She is split into two persons: one who possesses certain but finally secret knowledge of the nuclear catastrophe, and the other who denies it and, in both eagerness and despair, seeks to preserve a semblance of family peace so they can spend one more pleasant day together. The end is deception: "Yes, so it will be, and surely it was otherwise for Cassandra only because she had no husband and no children whom she had to deceive as I now deceive my husband and my children, even though it would be more logical to say, there you have it, you must die, why didn't you believe me. But I don't say this, and at the end of this long day it has come to the point where I deceive myself as well" (p. 77). Ingeborg Bachmann depicts women who are victims of men and have no luck, but who at the same time keep on trying to hide their desperate situation from the men in order to spare *them* pressure and guilt.[18] Through poor vision or discreet averting of the eyes, they protect themselves as well as the men from unpleasant reality.

It is against this background that men have been able to carry out their ride into disaster, their moral bankruptcy and corruption. Women have upheld the fiction that everything has a meaning – that meaning is the staff of life. The important thing is to believe in something. Belief in meaning fosters life and accomplishments; it gives strength. But the search for meaning is also a search for servitude and guideposts, a search for a mission which we long to fulfill, and thus also a search for someone to give orders, for instructions, for handicaps and dependency.

So what can "demoralizing" mean? The morality whose principles women are not supposed to abandon, or don't want to, has become the counterpart and correlative to the most brutal kind of immorality and meanness. This morality we can only refuse. If we prohibit ourselves from naming facts which are in this sense "demoralizing," then we are collaborating. For long enough we have not spoken the truth: out of shame or tact, to spare ourselves the spiteful laughter of those who have always known that women were no threat to them, or else so as not to get hurt. But the truth is reasonable.[19]

So we are lying to ourselves when we cling to the image of woman as a mere victim of patriarchal domination. Yet the uncovering of this lie does not acquit men; that is not at all the point.[20] We are accustomed to understanding all weakness and inadequacy, all thoughtlessness and limitation, all powerlessness as *results* of those relations which force women to be as they are: objects of history, modeling clay with which men can do anything they like. Thus the feminist explanation for women's invisibility in history and their relative ineffectiveness in the present is always that women were not permitted to influence cultural and political processes; women have roles and behavior patterns assigned to them; women are saddled with the burdens of reproduction; women are obstructed; women are injured, assimilated, abused, excluded. Women have not been allowed to determine for themselves. Decisions have been made for them.

This passive understanding of female behavior and female existence discriminates against *us.* Necessary as those cries of indignation were, they are not free of ideology. They contain self-justifications which falsify reality or grasp it superficially and analyze it inaccurately. They contain our own contribution to female powerlessness.

If we acknowledge "patriarchal relations" as the determinant of our behavior, then in an objectivistic dullness and stupidity of thought, we restrict our capacity to refuse to be determined. And this is exactly the intention.

The ideology that men act and woman are acted *upon,* or that society sets conditions to which women are *subjected,* is one of the manifestations of our complicity. We define women as objects and victims, the very images of women which are always before our eyes. The eternally willing, long-suffering wife and mother who sacrifices her wishes to the survival and peace of the family; the overtaxed, doubly-burdened woman whose life is caught between various unpostponable tasks; the woman with equal rights who gives away her identity so she can benefit from male privilege – all are victims. All endure evil and injustice, all are forced to share this fate, all painfully give up something which they need for themselves – their energies, their work, their identity – because without this costly gift to patriarchy they could not survive.

These sacrifices are painful but unnecessary, and they derive no meaning from being painful. The suffering they cause is meaningless. It does not issue in protest and life-affirmation, but rather in deformation: taking the world as it is, perhaps not actively increasing the misery, but still being prepared to suffer personally from the surrounding injustice. Victims are inconsequential; they do not have the morality that is imputed to them. And they are ineffectual; they do not admonish, or bear witness. They simply cease to exist one day. "Victim – a favorite word in the language of war."[21]

The ideological justification for female powerlessness, weakness, conformity, and finally also for female brutality reflects an interest in exoneration whose analysis until now has fallen victim to one of the many thought-prohibitions of feminism.

We brought this willingness to exonerate to everything that women did and thought. We were in the habit of regarding certain tendencies within the women's movement which appeared suspect to us as born of necessity: for example, the cult of motherhood and femininity, the concept of female self-realization through childbirth and motherhood; the retreat into the private life of relationships along with the underlying conviction that the talents of the female guardians of life need only be transferred to society at large to produce a more humane order. We were used to understanding such derailments as a reaction to intensifying social crises with their special effect on women, to economic setbacks, to the contraction of the labor market and of job possibilities for women, to general political repression, to shrinking tolerance for deviations, outbursts, and so-called alternative life styles. Shrugging our shoulders lamely, we declared ourselves content with these explanations.

For many women, the more menacing the outside world, and the more invisible and hopeless the results of our struggles for a political homeland and against the contemptuous logic of the ruling powers, the more burdensome becomes the idea of any engagement outside the home. They rediscover in private their special talents for contentment and comfort – which evidently failed to materialize in their ventures outside. In their memories, resistance and refusal became identical with stress. And staying at home doesn't require them to learn much of anything new.

The fiction that our own familiar and imperfect home can be made all warm and cozy, that the world exists only as our own creation – reducing reality to meaninglessness – can be sustained quite well for a time. That our own microcosm contains much of interest is not to be doubted; each of us can spend a great deal of time there. But retreating to the seemingly free realm of imaginative action, escaping to imaginary islands – these are symptoms of the survival of slaves.

All of this can be justified. Even the retreat is defended – without disturbing the circumstances themselves – by the hopeful theory, as abstract as it is empty, that social developments necessarily and naturally move in tidal rhythms. Thus a phase of expansion and progress in the women's movement is being followed by a phase of calm, stagnation, and turning inward.

But this simply is not so; I consider this view a considerate whitewashing of incompetence. For instance, the vague involvement with spiritual and mystical thought and the uncritical inhalation of astrological teachings about the personality, which are taken out of their historical context, and which were spawned by male brains; the indiscriminate pilfering of world history, lifting scraps from religions, from philosophies, from ways of life which have arisen in every culture but our own – and for that reason are no less polluted by patriarchal myths and cannot simply be appropriated, at least not with impunity – these are retreats into a realm that only appears to be without consequences, a realm in which nothing is verifiable and refutable, and everything is arbitrary and diffuse. Likewise the cult of self-preoccupation, this egocentrism of the body, along with the celebration of something we originally protested against, our femininity, now occupied as a "utopian" alternative and given the highest value – all this cannot be right. The result is not only a "theoretical muddle," but also an unliveable, perverse way of life.[22]

Certainly it is no wonder that we don't exactly feel at home inside our own cultural four walls and that it sometimes becomes unbearable to be in our own skins. But escapist borrowings from foreign cultures are superficial and naive when they are accompanied by the erroneous prejudice that there we don't have to deal with the devastating traces of patriarchal interests and can spare ourselves the exertion of demystification. The male myth-makers are simply harder to recognize from afar; they deceive us in disguise. If we want to become clear about ourselves and our complicity, then we must at least begin to work – equally and thoroughly – on our own history and culture. Patriarchal colonization has not spared women; it grows in our heads like an abscess.[23] It would be a good idea to recognize it, to render it harmless, and to see how to live without it.

Belief in the lawfulness of history and in the necessary rhythms of revolution certainly belongs to the realm of illusion. This does not mean, however, that it is not helpful to know more about the prehistory and tradition of certain ineradicable female stereotypes which are currently experiencing a revival. I have in mind a pattern of behavior that many women, at least in bourgeois society, especially treasure – introspection – and another that, for a considerably longer time, they have mastered particularly well – suffering.

In nineteenth-century history we can see that it was the realm of inwardness which women were allowed to enter with impunity, especially if they were content to remain there and renounce any interest in extending their passion for discovery to the outside world, and if they were willing to become those sentimental creatures, those "geniuses of the soul" whose satisfaction lay in developing ultrasensitive antennae for their own feelings and for their immediate world, centered on husband and children.[24] At any rate, it is hardly an advance now for women to insist upon this inwardness and apply themselves to it intensely, as if it were a new discovery. It is in fact the desired feminine self-limitation, the prescribed disease, especially for women of the middle classes. Its function is quite simply the exclusion of women from the corridors of power. To sink into inwardness, the only luxury of obedient servants, has led not to maturity and balance but to silencing and disappearance. What is new, in any case, is that many women now persist in this exile and endorse it themselves, whereas this used to be the doing of the male manufacturers of the split between inwardness and action.[25]

This ghetto of the soul has not brought us happiness. Furthermore, it has systematically prevented the development of our competence. When we look at the suffering caused by enforced ghettoization, which was especially destructive to women of the bourgeois class in the last century, the retreat on the part of women today begins to look cynical. Then, women longed for more action, more vision, more experience, to look out beyond the confines of their female lives: "Millions [of women] are condemned to a stiller doom than mine, and millions are in silent revolt against their lot. . . . Women are supposed to be very calm generally. . . . They need exercise for their faculties and a field for their efforts. . . . they suffer from too rigid a restraint, too absolute a stagnation. . . . It is thoughtless to condemn them, or laugh at them, if they seek to do more or learn more than custom has pronounced necessary for their sex" (Charlotte Brontë, *Jane Eyre*). Fortunately, this author of the early nineteenth century has been spared the chorus of laments which her sisters have struck up a hundred and fifty years later. We have not been able to chase away the ghosts of her sorrow. Women still suffer from "rigid restraint" and "absolute stagnation." The only difference seems to be that women's imaginations have now openly acquired a taste for this suffering, or at least they are still bound to suffering and to the inner catastrophes of their personal histories (for example, in feminist novels from the seventies to the present, almost without exception; in women's encounter and therapy groups, and so on).

The suffering is still in the private realm. Under the sex-specific division of labor into suffering and action, women have put so much energy and emotional intensity into the longterm experience of suffering that their identity is bound up in it. Ultimately, they seem to have gotten caught up in regressive self-dramatization, as if it were a kind of home. In the meantime, the chords of powerlessness and passivity sound so natural, so common, so perfect – and often so sour, so offended, so tough, and so devoid of hate.

When Jutta Heinrich exposes her suffering in this murderers' time, the sound is different. She cannot bear "the luxury of not looking" and "not thinking through to the end."[26] She dares to look the horror of reality full in the face and to resist, at incalculable emotional risk, the temptations of a gentle consolation born of repression. Suffering is passionate. And when Christa Wolf asks what this culture has actually done to deserve surviving, and when she suggests that "the only thing that can help and save us now is what really isn't done" and that the point now must be to "think what really isn't thought," then this suffering becomes daring and demanding.[27]

There is no way around the need to see clearly, without cheating, and to renounce all illusions. The strength produced by illusions is a miserable crutch; it leads to despair and self-contempt.

Our only way is out of deception into un-deception: to have the courage to look things in the face and not be on the lookout for perspectives or developments where there are none. We must radically reject every superficial consolation. If women were finally to become nihilists in this sense, it would be a revolutionary act.

We crave life, not death. For this reason let us strike "hope" and "meaning" from our vocabulary. They are saturated with lies, with acts of violence and repeated anesthetizing. We can't clean them out and fill them with new contents; the old husks would instantly attract the old poison. It is not enough to redefine and rebaptize – to renovate, but to retain the old blueprint.

Such a separation does not leave a legacy of despair. On the contrary, it frees us from the Sisyphean labor of untangling, sorting, unloading, detoxifying – only to end up sitting in front of the same pile of garbage and murderous, or empty, tricks.

Nevertheless, for many such a parting can apparently be conceived only as fatal. "What's positive about this? No one can live without hope!" But an understanding of our life as hope-less, meaning-less and dis-illusioned is life-threatening only if we relapse into conformity, into weariness, inertia, flippancy, and self-poisoning, the products of continual powerlessness. In other words, only if we relapse into the normalcy of female self-contempt and suffering.

To live without hope should mean that we concentrate on the life that remains to us, on this present existence. Certainly I'm not so stupid as to claim that once our five senses apprehend the world we've understood everything. But we ought now to hold onto what is certain. We should *qualify* for this life. It is irreplaceable. And if we revolt against the scandal being perpetrated on this earth, let it be for only one reason: because life still contains uncontaminated moments. As long as we are still in a position to experience them, we can draw strength from this life and from the endorsement of ourselves and our protest that expresses this declaration of our belief in life. The most reliable resistance comes from the ability to live – unreconciled with our self-justifications, and unreconciled with our complicity.

4

LOVE AND LIES: "MY BELOVED CHILDREN"

A devout National Socialist, German officer, and Evangelical priest wrote letters from the front to his two daughters before his "hero's death" in 1941. He was my father. I do not release these letters now out of some belated revenge. They are historical documents, pieces of political history and women's history and more than a personal legacy.

I was four and my sister was eight when the letters reached us. Each letter begins with: "My beloved children" or "My dearest children" and ends with "Your dearest Daddy." The touching parts of these letters used to affect me deeply, although I scarcely have any concrete memories of the person who was my father. In any case, he remained present after his death, mediated through intense ties to my mother and sister, in the form of a picture. Nothing in this picture could be changed, corrected, or verified. It was static: my father, the ideal person, the absolutely good person who seemed to be missing everywhere and always and who now after his death looked down on us from heaven day and night and accompanied us in everything we did.

The letters were stored in a hand-painted wooden box by my sister's bed. From the time I was able to read, I read them often, always secretly, and always the writing was blurred by tears. I spoke with no one about it, not till decades later.

My sister, who, like me, on the fiftieth anniversary of the so-called fascist seizure of power, set to work on our common property, separated the "subjective intentions" of the letters from their "objective content," dividing her father into two persons: the enemy whose head was filled with National Socialist ideology, and the loving human being. The latter was to be preserved in memory, unsullied by his fascist ideas and deeds. In order to preserve him, "it became difficult for me *not* to forget."[1] My sister has happy childhood memories of her father to lose, in contrast to me − I was too small. I used to envy her for this. Today I feel perhaps less hurt than she when once again I lay out before me the messages left to us.

To judge people by two different yardsticks, one political and the other personal, to split a person into human and inhuman, to discriminate between "objective" and "subjective" action, protects us from separations which we think we won't be able to endure or answer for. This applies not only to the dead. With the help of such dissociation, we can allow the physical or psychic proximity of people from whom we would instantly retreat, whom we would avoid or resist, if they did not happen to be our father, had they not entered our lives as friend, lover, husband. Such divisions are helpful constructions through which we try, in spite of refusal, repugnance, and contradiction, to hold on to relationships. With the same mechanisms of self-deception women refuse to identify the man who tortures them with the man they stay with. "The man who beats me is not the man I love."[2] The denial of reality spares us the decision to separate.

The dichotomies of subjective-objective, personal-political are soothing, guarantees of continuity, gentle and agreeable, for they help to postpone breakups and break-throughs. They are preventive medicine, relief from pain.

We can choose to assent to illusion and deception as helpful medicine: a smart person does not take a good look, or at least looks from a distance, that is, grasps at every means to gloss over reality. Thus all veils, touch-ups, and illusory images are legitimate. Or we can subscribe to the doctrine of cynical reason and grit our teeth in the presence of reality and pain, approach life with a tough and penetrating spirit, know it all, and simply hang in. In the first case we do not look, in the second case we look without conse-quences. In both cases we justify not having to separate.

My sister describes the situation in which the letters reached us:

> When the war began and my father was drafted, a gap opened for us. The centerpiece of our former life, our father, was far away, accessible only through let-ters; he was exposing himself to danger (in order to

protect us; we – women and children – had to prove ourselves on the home front). For me as the oldest it often went like this: "You are Daddy's representative now. Show what you can do!" The parish community now consisted of my mother, my sister and me, my grandmother, our maid, and the parish nurse. In addition to this a substitute for my father moved in with us. We did not take him seriously because he was a man "hanging around the house" while my father was out at the front putting his life on the line. . . . I already possessed the qualities typical of a Christian, bourgeois-educated, fascist childhood: boundless trust in father, the moral need to assume responsibility and to prove myself, great faith in words, great capacity for enthusiasm and illusion, and the seeds of political conformity – namely, saying yes, going along, and obeying and believing unconditionally. My father's letters from the front fell on fertile ground. (p. 10)

All the letters attest to our utter deference as girls to the concept of total war. The central appeal of the letter is directed to our proving ourselves on the home front, to our faithful assistance on this side of the total war.

(Western front, 5/11/1940)

My dearest child,
The great battle has now begun here in the west against the French and English, and your Daddy probably won't be able to be at home with you for your birthday. But you shouldn't be sad about this, for the Fatherland is the greatest thing in

> *this world, the greatest shrine. . . . We must all serve it*
> *gladly, and if the Führer calls us away from Mommy and the*
> *children, then we obey willingly. . . . You must be very happy*
> *and proud that your Daddy is a German soldier and you*
> *yourself are also a bit of a soldier, because you are making*
> *such a great sacrifice to the Fatherland and the Führer on*
> *your birthday in giving your Daddy away to be on the front*
> *instead of with you. Anyone who makes a sacrifice to his*
> *Fatherland is a soldier, even if he's a little girl.*

This is the essence of every letter: rehearsing us in soldierly morality for girls. We are integrated into, not excluded from, the great tasks of the nation. Technically, according to the letters' wording, the same ideals apply to girls our age as to the men at war. Girls simply achieve them in another place, at home, and thus with a different kind of behavior. This creates solidarity, proximity, and the consciousness of equality and importance; this complementary home-front soldiery makes the people invincibly strong. "You too are helping the Führer! You too are helping! You are indispensable!"

The National Socialist Führer demanded of those who did not or could not go to war but stayed at home and were not persecuted that they make their stand just as rigidly and dutifully as the front-line soldiers. Women and children who do this need not feel inferior to the heroes at the front; they are assured that they are equally valuable, that they don't need to be ashamed. For they have it in their power either to strengthen the backbones of the men at the front, or to break them. It's up to them whether or not the soldiers will prove themselves, to a man, to be fit for action, whether or not they will make it through the "awful work of facing the

enemy, facing death." "You are all front-line fighters. Only
the position the Führer gives you is different; the duty and
the responsibility are the same, and everyone must know
that it depends on every single person."[3]

Women and children are drawn into the great goal of
renewing the national community – against the background
of the enemies Judaism and Communism – and also drawn
into the great male event, the great war. The propaganda
campaign of Rudolf Hess, "Women help to win," once again
made clear to women from 1941 on the indispensability and
importance of the home front to the external front "out
there," and their own moral power and duty. Without
women men could not even take up arms, for women hand
the weapons to them; they produce the personal legitimation
of the male war ethic and the unconditional willingness to
hang in "till the last victory." This requires the ideologically
upright posture of the wife and her daughters, and their
cooperative, indefatigable, and flexible work.

If the war is represented as a difficult yet brilliant
operation, then a constant effort must be made so that the
home front does not feel its enforced and permitted abstinence, its nonparticipation in the male war, its staying at
home, as a deficit. And an even more difficult psychological
operation has to succeed: namely, the dressing up and glossing
over of the loss of the men themselves (who indeed consti-
tuted "the woman's world" and were everything to them,
not just in the propaganda), of their death on the front – so
that the bereaved wives, mothers, daughters, and sisters don't
throw all their willingness to fulfill National Socialist duties
overboard. Their resolve must prevail beyond death, prevail
in spite of death. The duty of renunciation includes death.

This in fact is the real test of how genuine and dependable their war effort is.

Digression: A Reader for Girls

In a National Socialist reader for girls I expected to find stories about moral and child-bearing women, women happy to be mothers; stories about family happiness; girls aspiring to the same condition; women, far removed from any historical connection, assigned to the fictitious elementary sphere – as they are portrayed in National Socialist art. Material, in other words, for a portrait of National Socialist children and women. This proved to be wrong. The 180 or so stories, songs, poems, fairytales, aphorisms, and anecdotes in this girls' reader which still sits on my bookshelf (an example with no claim to being representative), on over 250 closely printed pages, address with very few exceptions not the subject of women and girls, but men, fathers, sons, boys.[4] They are primarily about communicating a certain image of men to the girls: men and boys who are marching, who are giving their lives for the Führer, who met the Führer personally, whose hand the Führer shook, whom the Führer looked straight in the eye, who sing "The World Belongs to the Leaders," who heroically take part in aerial attacks, who free comrades being held by Communists, who sacrifice themselves and cheerfully pour out their blood, who carry blood-spangled flags, who die on the high seas and have contempt for all who have fears or doubt. Small boys who dare to take on a gander (in contrast to their bigger sisters), boys who abhor sympathy, who make no "squeamish feminine gestures," even when their well-meaning father throws them from their beds into the snow or secretly stuffs the little child's pushcart with rocks, so that the child learns to exert himself at an early age. "The smallest person can do wonders, if he only has the courage for it." Stories of male heroes from the German past, of Prince Eugene the noble knight, of Frederick William I of Prussia, of Frederick the Great, who was at war with the whole world, of General Zieten, the cavalry general of Frederick the Great, of Fridericus Rex, of Andreas Hofer's heroic battle against the French, of German heroes who "thirsted after French blood," of the Hindenburg cadets and the SA storm troopers in battle; reports from wars with the English in South Africa and the Russians in the Crimea: brave men, cheerful men, adventurous and level-headed, comradely and helpful, radiant and steady, excited and confident. The illustrations in this girls' reader show the marching storm troopers, a Panzer division, Lützow's wild pursuit with horse and sword, Siegfried with a decapitated horse's head over his shoulder, and finally a sower and a young rabbit.

The training here is not aimed toward outlining the features of the female personality – or better, its essence – with their specific National Socialist markings. Much more prominent is the production of all-embracing identification with the war, which means with those who wage it and carry it out, with men. What principally matters is the production of a relationship: women and girls should direct their feelings, thoughts, and interests toward these men. If they do so, it is unnecessary to spell out the particulars of which qualities are supposed to help them "relate" to these men, revere them, dream of them, find them desirable. If the first step succeeds, the second naturally follows: to focus their emotional energy and imagination on the combination man/war/ hero and then naturally to see their entire happiness in winning such a man, keeping him, taking care of him, belonging to him, serving him, and subjecting themselves to him, for otherwise he can't be that figure deserving of adoration, a German hero, on both a large and a small scale.

This background may explain why in my girls' reader (intended for sixth-graders, published in 1939), the image of the Jewish enemy, male or female, barely appears.[5] This at a time when — even before the Kristallnacht of November 9, 1938 — the politics of expulsion was fully underway: already about 250,000 Jews had been forced to emigrate from or flee Germany, the first concentration camps had been set up (Dachau, Buchenwald, Sachsenburg, Sachsenhausen, and Esterwegen), and terrorist acts against Jews were no secret.[6] Nevertheless the primary enemy of the German man is pictured as a "bloodthirsty pack" of Communists, this "death plague" that insidiously attacks the peaceful unsuspecting storm troopers on the street. I found only one direct anti-Semitic comment: a "Communist Jewess," leader of a "band of criminals," who murders Horst Wessel, the composer of the National Socialist hymn "Die Fahne hoch," and goes on to celebrate her victory with schnapps and beer (p. 243).

Given the intention of this collection of texts addressed to eleven-year-old girls, the idealization and whitewashing of the German male, it may have seemed unprofitable to the publishers to impress on the girls' minds the actions and intentions of the National Socialists regarding Jews. These might have disturbed their image of men. What's communicated to the girls is above all positive. Everything German is noble and good, "German to the core": the German Reich, the German people, the German earth, the German person, even the German animal – animals (in foreign lands) "speak German." Everything is harmonious and everything turns out well – for the Germans – every time; the German man is infallible and unbeatable.

The few stories about girls or women are after this relationship, this combination. They are about female self-sacrifice for the male war and national expansion, about hatred of everything non-German; this is never an abstract political idea, for the sacrifice succeeds by way of these wonderful persons who are carrying out the great war operation as their way of life.

From women and girls this round-the-clock work requires tireless industry and courage. The exhortations to loyalty and stamina addressed to women are intended not to motivate their personal battle for survival, but rather to insure national survival at home for the material and psychic strengthening of the men fighting far away. The old and infirm, by offering themselves, give their lives the only meaning left: for example, a grandmother bravely sets her own house on fire and with it everything she owns in order to warn the villagers celebrating on the ice of a coming storm. Without her sacrifice all would have died. And without her sacrifice this grandmother would have been worthless and superfluous. To sacrifice without expecting thanks or reward is the ethic of these women; humility – for the point of their service to save the men – is their victory. "Johanna had to do something for the brave ones. . . . The inactivity to which she was condemned pained her deeply. Johanna envied every cavalryman." Finally she collected cartridges in her apron and braved a hail of bullets to distribute them, to the German heroes of course, without fear for her life. "Around her the fighting men fell, she did not waver. She was undaunted. The rain of bullets did not trouble her" (p. 207). After the great deed had succeeded, and her men had won, she had only one wish: not to be recognized. And no one did recognize her. Women are supposed to seek out a task actively and accomplish it both fearlessly and anonymously.

To find a task with which to make a contribution to the common goal with one's own means was the idea when the ten- to fourteen-year-old girls of the German girls' league in a city district of Cologne independently developed a plan to collect kitchen scraps at doorsteps every day so as to feed seventy pigs on a farm without cost. If everyone did this, then over two million pigs and three and a half million hundredweights of meat and bacon per year could be produced through nothing but the unpaid girls' labor. What's required is resourcefulness and toughness. And also a specifically female disdain for boys who are only showoffs or cowards.

All this assumes an intense personal as well as general and abstract relationship to the male, and identification with his goals, which are technically also female goals. This female soldiery demands not only preparedness for the later battle of childbirth; it requires a lifelong fundamental psychic readiness for cheerful renunciation and willing sacrifice, wherever they might or might not be needed, depending on the progress of the war. In order for this to work, lies must not be seen as lies, and restrictions and renunciation must not be seen as forced acts, but as marks of nobility, as "crowns of honor."

The exhortative and caring letters of my father formulate what such a soldiery demands of little girls:

The Obligation to be Sweet and Good

(Front line, 2/15/40)

I was so happy to get your dear letter and thanked the dear Lord for giving me such dear little children. How nice that is! Now Daddy can be a much better and more joyful soldier because he knows that he is fighting for such dear, good children and watches to see that no bad enemy hurts his little children. If his children were badly behaved, then Daddy would not be so glad to be a soldier. For one cannot tolerate so much hardship for bad children.

(In the bunker of the front line, 2/27/40)

You dear good children, think always about the many thousands of soldiers who are out on the front for you and are having a very rough time. They are doing this so that things will be good for you. A child who knows this surely won't be naughty.

(In the big forest like Hansel and Gretel's, 3/26/40)

Do you see the brook and the birds and the Easter bunny?

The sweet little birds told me that you are sweet. This made me very happy.

Think about the soldiers . . . and be sweet and brave.

To be sweet, a charge that is missing from no letter, was a meta-concept on the scale of the rules of female wartime behavior. To be sweet and good was synonymous with the soldierly female code of behavior. But beyond this, being sweet created a specific tone for the implementation, the praxis, of following rules; being sweet meant also having a sense of how everything was to be transformed – namely, very carefully and lovingly, very peacefully, very attentively, inventively, and touchingly. Here a trivialized version of nature played an important supporting role – the little flowers, the little animals, are allies, all in this together – as did homey creativity, the painting of little pictures, the making of lovely little handicrafts, the singing of songs, the little surprises, the spreading of joy. The call to be sweet was joined to sacrifices of the soldiers on the front to give it a place in the total war.

The Obligation to be Happy

(Arnicourt, France, 2/23/41)

It is very cold here again, and the snow is deep. But the little flowers are still growing. So we should always be glad and hope, even when it's hard and we want to cry. All the houses here are destroyed. There aren't any people or children either. They all fled last year, when the war was raging here. So it's especially nice that the dear Lord lets flowers grow amidst all the destruction and death. But life, which shows itself in the little flowers too, will win out. So then how can we despair and be sad. This you must tell your dear Mommy too.

Be cheerful, all of you. . . . You must never be sad . . . are you still cheerful?

Mommy wrote she was often sad because Daddy isn't there. If we're sad we get sick.

(On the return march, St. Aillant sûr Tholen, 7/6/40)

We have to ask God to give us a courageous and brave heart so that we don't cry and lose heart in unhappiness. Even little children have to learn to be brave, not to cry, and always to be gay.

We were supposed to be happy about everything, always be gay and bring joy to everyone. So it was frequently though reluctantly mentioned that our mother was sad and we had to do everything to make her happy. We should lighten her load with our consideration, concern, and accommodation. We were responsible for helping her to bear loneliness, confinement, strain, and fear. We should sing her lullabies, pick her flowers, read her poems; secretly invite friends she enjoyed; set the coffee table to surprise her. She was portrayed as almost younger and more helpless than we were, as if she had not yet sufficiently mastered the abilities which the female sex of the future – represented by us – was to acquire, a sex in which "joy is alive in her heart, which finds in this joy the strength throughout life to make sacrifices for her natural duty."[7] Simply to make sacrifices was not enough; they had to be made cheerfully and devoutly, with body and soul. Bitter or resigned sacrifices did not count as sacrifices.

The Obligation to Endure

(On the return march, 7/6/40)

> *We are marching back to Germany. This makes us very happy. But, dear children, the marching is very hard. We are marching day and night and night and day. We have to get up at 1 or 2 or 3 A.M. We march without a rest. Every day 40 or 50 km. Many soldiers are sick again. Daddy is not sick, but his legs hurt him very much. . . . We thank the dear Lord that our children have a bed and that the Führer Adolf Hitler has seen to it that our children and their Mommies can stay at home. . . . Yes, there is much unhappiness in the world. . . . Think always of the German soldiers who have to fight and march so much with many wounds and with bloody feet. They do not cry. . . . Think of this and be sweet and brave . . .*

The great German *perseverance* was realized by enduring despite pain, sickness, and overexertion, despite death, despite reluctance, despite sympathy with the enemy injured – naturally only the women and children – enduring despite feelings of melancholy about the harm inflicted; enduring in the face of all the signals which made each and every one unambiguously aware that something physically and psychically adverse, perverse, was happening to people. This adversity, which was truly unendurable, was robbed of its adverseness by the fact that it was endured. In this way it turned into a reward, into a moral good. Whoever endured the unreasonable had scored a moral victory and was trustworthy and righteous.

And *everyone* could be such a hero – the kind of person who overcomes himself, who casts himself off, who doesn't trust his own experiences, who perceives himself and takes himself seriously only as an instrument. The more difficult the conditions under which it functions, the better the instrument.

The Obligation to Obey

(In the bunker, front line, 2/27/40)

You write that you love your Daddy so and want so much to see him again and he should come home on vacation. Oh yes, how much I would like to come. But we soldiers must fight and defend Germany, the Fatherland, and protect all the dear mommies, grandparents, and little children. So we can't go on vacation very often. Our Führer needs all the soldiers. Not one can be spared, and only when the general or captain allows can we come to Mommy and to the children. We can't just go when we want, we must always obey. The dear Lord has commanded the soldiers to obey always. No one may do things his own way. This is our duty. So I can't tell you when I'll come see you again. But you may always pray to the dear Lord that your Daddy can come on leave again and find you safe and sound. I am very sure that the dear Lord will listen to you because he's especially fond of children.

The hero, even the male hero, our model, our point of reference, was not a self-sufficient decisive type. In fact he was dependent like the children. His greatness did not lie in his self-sufficiency, but in the perfection of his subordination and submission, in the thorough shutting down of his own will. The spirit of the servant was freed from doubt about who and what are served by obedience and obligation, or about their meaning or content. Such questions were also of no concern to the male heroes. They were relieved by the division of labor. They had already decided. And when we obeyed, we were loved.

The Obligation to Be Grateful and Proud

> We are still marching in the dead of night. If you ever wake up in the night, then you must think: now my Daddy is marching, and you must be proud. . . .

> You must be happy and proud that your father is a German soldier. . . .

> Think always of the German soldiers who must fight and march so much, with many wounds and with bloody feet. They do not cry. . . .

> Your Daddy is glad to be a soldier when he knows that he can defend such dear little children from the wicked enemies.

> The Führer is having a very rough time and is doing everything for the German children, so that life will finally be good for them and they can do much good.

The production of the feeling of pride in male soldiery could be achieved only through the relationship between girl and man, woman and man. The goal was to increase female value, not by the action of the girls themselves but by the representatives of the male side of the war. This increase in worth was to be achieved through heightening female self-esteem (still rather pathetic), through the advantage of personal alliance with one of the heroes as well as general participation in their struggle, and finally through profiting from the war as a whole, since it took place exclusively in the interest of the children and all the male suffering and sacrifice was for the children. Our value was increased because men were fighting and dying for us. In return, we were to accept the offered relationship, or rather the commanded relationship: be thankful to us, be proud of us, for we are doing all this for you! Our part included fulfilling our own duties, especially since these were unequal, simpler and more harmless. While we slept in our own beds, our only task was to think of the marching soldiers with the bleeding feet. After such a night of bad conscience, to get up in the morning and *not* obey, *not* come up with a great new idea for some sweet thing to do today – how hardened such a child would have to be!

To involve girls in the female version of soldierly values, no calculated pedagogical manipulation was necessary. An effective means was the merciless and normal interplay of care with the emotional feedback of the one cared for: he has the feeling of loving someone, he *needs* the feeling of loving someone; those that he loves want to be loved by him, he *needs* the certainty that they love him.

Kindly feelings toward children and women served the function of enabling a man psychically to endure the daily state of wartime emergency and to counter the daily experience of murder and fear with something wholesome and clean – and to legitimate his own murders as well as his own hardships. The everyday emotions of war, the proofs and assurances of love, had to be combined with lies about reality, for those who were loved were not allowed to gain any insight into the reality of events in the war, except in a twisted version. Insight into reality might have shaken the feelings of those who were supposed to return love. So the lie becomes a supplementary value of the love. The warrior must under all circumstances remain worthy of love; what he does must be seen as good by those whom he loves and who are supposed to love him.

The decisive means to this end was the intensity of the relationship, the constant assurance of love and protection and the assurance of the indispensability of the child to the common goal. Not only the demand to be strong, be good, be sweet, be brave, but the constant assurance that you *are* good and sweet, you are my support, you are the reason to endure hardships and to accept death, and not only I love you, but so do the deer and the birds – as long as you go along.

The guarantee of love was not unconditional; it was unmistakable how I was to be and not to be. There was no doubt. The strong assurances of love in the letters had the effect of a wall built around or over us. We were walled in right where we were, rooted to the spot. The work of building this wall and the giant political weight that depended on it, the unconditional hope that was placed in us, favored an appearance of stability that was tied to the person who gave the assurances and to his characteristics: to a man, an authority figure, an infallible, inaccessible man – God, father, man all in one. It fostered dependence on an "absolute." It was perfectly suited to creating a false or broken relationship to oneself.

For what does a child do when it is suggested to her by the representatives of the "good" that she is strong, sweet, brave, happy, and so on, but who at the same time has the opposite experience of herself every day. I, for example, was shy, skittish, and nervous, often unhappy and very often unfriendly, a so-called difficult child. All the qualities which were required I didn't really have. They were alien; I could only attempt them. I seemed to be recognized by attributes that I didn't at all possess, but were presented to me as original and my own, and coupled with the eternal offer of the good father's love. In reality I was afraid of a thousand things; of mice, frogs, and storms, especially of strange people; I wouldn't walk out the door alone, didn't want to go to kindergarten, didn't know a single child except my sister for an entire year; I was cross-eyed and already wore glasses at three, a physical defect. My father was frightening to me. I admired my sister. She was really the way we were supposed to be. She lived an exemplary life. And although I did not meet the conditions, she was the one who never put conditions on her patient and unshakable affection for me – one of the contradictions that were my salvation.

In her unpublished memoirs, which she finished at the age of seventy-seven, my mother writes of that time when I was secretly reading the letters: "With all the sorrow I worried so about the children. . . . I felt deeply connected with them. I wanted to be near them constantly. We needed each other very much." And later: "We were always . . . called 'the three sisters.' . . . We lived, like most families in those years, in a household of women only. . . . We war widows were in any case not invited anywhere by married couples.

We stood completely outside. Single women were more or less avoided. We war widows banded together even tighter. . . . I had found these women in the immediate neighborhood. We met often and regularly, kept close together, helped each other where we could. We understood one another. These friendships meant enormously much to us and they have lasted over many decades."[8]

This attitude of my mother's, her natural, unobtrusive, and unconditional affection for us when we were children and also her allies in a world scarcely accessible to us, her interest and participation in the lives of others, and the shared experience of being an outsider to those normal "complete" families, which never attracted me – all this was a counter-experience for me that stood in stark contrast to the glorious, contradictory, brutal world of the letters.

If you could not experience in your own self the contradictions between big words, demands, and assurances on the one hand and the reality that deviated from them on the other, you had scarcely any chance of feeling them at all. For children – at any rate in the context of a life like ours, in which war was a dark memory not to be discussed – there was almost no opportunity for us to uncover the unending lies and distortions.

(Front line, 2/15/40)

Last Sunday evening Daddy went to check on the machine guns in a bunker way up in front. Suddenly there was a frightful bang. Red and blue flames shot out, splinters of iron and stone whizzed around. The soldiers ran away in the first shock, but Daddy brought them right back again. Just think, the bunker was hit by five rounds that went into the room where we were standing. And one soldier lay badly wounded on the ground with a round in the chest, another was hit in the arm, a third in the leg. Daddy got only four pieces of shrapnel in his face. . . . My dear children, it is very serious when one sees a good friend . . . lying on the ground bleeding. We bandaged the soldier and brought him in back. . . . That he was not dead is thanks to the grace of God, otherwise his dear mother would have had to cry. And it is also thanks to the grace of God that Daddy was hardly hit. I know that it is because you all pray for Daddy, the dear Lord is with me now, and his angels turn the bullets away. . . .

(Front line, Westwall, 11/25/39)

Your dear Mommy has surely already told you that Daddy is in the most forward position with the German soldiers, every day he sees the French. They have blue and greenish brown jackets on and they fire often. But they don't hit anything. . . .

(In a bunker on the front line, 2/27/40)

When the French shoot, we shoot too. Soon we want to attack them too, so that they will finally leave us alone and we can at last come home to our children. . . .

(Undated)

Today is Sunday and the French are not shooting. So I can write you a little letter. I send greetings from the sweet little birds here. Robins and blackbirds. They have nothing to eat outside in the deep snow. So they come hopping to our bunker and we feed them. A little bird brought a greeting from you. . . . Also I send greetings from two beautiful white swans who flew over our position several days ago, and from many gray wild geese. They came from far away and have brothers and sisters near you on the North Sea. They said we should all not be sad that Daddy is not at home. For the angels are always flying back and forth and . . . sending large and small birds to cheer up B. and S. . . . I was so happy that the dear God gives us everything so that we are joyful. . . .

(2/23/41)

All the houses here are destroyed. There aren't any people or children either. They all fled last year, when the war was raging here. So it's especially nice that the dear Lord lets the flowers grow amidst all the destruction and all the death. . . .

(6/3/41)

What do you say to the great victory on the island of Crete? The German soldiers jumped out of the planes into the air and landed with parachutes, the way we did playing with the little parachute and the doll. Hopefully we will soon land in England, so that the war will be over and Daddy can come home again. . . .

(7/6/40)

*Daddy must lead the company. . . . Daddy has to see to it
that all the soldiers keep up and none collapses. . . . France
is a very beautiful land with wonderful mountains, valleys,
and meadows. There are ivy trees and laurel trees and chestnut forests. The villages are mostly destroyed from the battles.
Many refugees wander through the country, women and little
children. They were afraid of the shooting. Many children are
sick and cry. We help them. At night they have to sleep
outside. When they come home, they have no bed, for everything is destroyed. We thank the dear Lord that our children
have a bed. . . .*

We learned: The German soldiers are doing good in the war;
they never harm anyone; they help wounded deer and put
them by the warm stove; they feed starving animals.
Instead of: The German soldiers are carrying out mass murder.

We learned: It is sad and tragic that the beautiful French
countryside is destroyed and that children and women are
afraid and homeless.
Instead of: The German soldiers have destroyed the countryside and they are the ones that the French women and
children are afraid of.

We learned: The German soldiers help the French civilian
population.
Instead of: German soldiers are raping women and plundering
households.

We learned: The dear animals are all on the side of the German soldiers.
Instead of: The animals are suffering serious injuries from the war. Besides which they are not German allies.

We learned: The poor French children fled as the war raged.
Instead of: They fled from the Germans.

We learned: The flowers grow as a compensation for so many people having to die in the war.
Instead of: The flowers know no connection between their growth and human war. This reconciliation does not take place.

We learned: Victory (for instance, on Crete) is achieved like child's play and is fun like child's play.
Instead of: It means murdering people and subjugating a country.

We learned: German soldiers conquer a country in order to be able to be with their children again.
Instead of: German soldiers conquer a country out of the will to conquer and subjugate, a crime, not in order to do good for children.

We learned: Father is infallible and always superior.
Instead of: His negligence set off the trouble with the machine gun.

We learned: Father is braver than all the others. He is never weak.
Instead of: He is no different than any of the others.

We learned: The soldier friend stayed alive by the grace of God.
Instead of: He narrowly escaped death because they were fooling around with deadly weapons.

We learned: The death of the badly wounded man would have been bad because his mother would have wept.
Instead of: Every death in war is murder, even with no weeping mother.

We learned: Father was not hit because his children prayed for him. The angels turned the bullets away from him.
Instead of: He was lucky.

We learned: The French shoot a lot, but don't hit anything.
Instead of: The French killed 27,000 Germans and wounded 100,000 (Westwall 1940–41).

We learned: The French were the attackers; the Germans are forced to defend themselves for the sake of their children.
Instead of: The Germans attacked Belgium and France. The French army lost thirty divisions and almost its entire air force, in addition to 1.9 million prisoners.

We learned: Robins, blackbirds, and other birds love us and send greetings.
Instead of: They have different problems than we do. We do not interest them in the slightest.

We learned: The birds say we are good and healthy; they say we must not be sad, but brave.
Instead of: The unsuspecting birds do nothing of the kind.

Animals are not here to comfort us. They are not here for human beings at all. But they cannot protect themselves from the presumption that they are partners in human crime.

For children, reality is not a category which can be distinguished in any recognizable way from stories, fantasies, dreams, hoaxes, and deliberate lies. Little can be proven, almost everything is believed. Often they can't prove anything until it's too late. It's only in retrospect that the lies devalue and vitiate the assurances of love.

What's dangerously normal about these letters is the *indivisibility* of love and lies. And so there is a temptation to extrapolate from their contents the so-called objective content, the so-called political function, and to separate these from the "private" feelings. But it is exactly the mixture of male war interests and loving feelings that make up their essence: being used by the one who loves you, not apart from his other actions, but for the sake of them.

5

THE LAST OUTBREAK
OF LOVE

n 1945 we arrived at Bethel Hospital, my mother, my
sister, and I, taken in out of Christian charity like many
other former inhabitants of regions in eastern Germany.
My brief childhood was already full of dreary impressions:
black-clad women who wept frequently, photos in our apartment of my father's grave in Russia, his soldier's cap on a
nail over my mother's bed, his wedding ring next to hers on
her right hand, and the burdensome feeling that to my mother
life consisted of a scarcely manageable pain that was never
to be touched upon. The smell of smoke in darkened Berlin
as we got off one of the last westbound trains from Pommern
at the Friedrichstrasse station. Low-flying planes on the way
to school, collapsing buildings which we saw burning on the
horizon from our cellar. The lamp in the kitchen covered in
black on the nights when we waited for the all-clear siren,
the muffled sound of the bomber squadron that glittered in
the sun of the blue May skies.

And now Bethel, and peace: bomb craters, some
twenty-five thousand of them, with birch saplings and clumps
of grass growing in them. My sister, whom I always took to
be so strong, keeling over waiting in the long shopping lines.
The people here seemed drearier than ever. On the streets,

on the woodland paths, in the post office, in the church, the sick, mostly epileptics, with their leather crash helmets and their faces bloated from bromine, their dragging gait, their sudden and expected screams, their convulsive movements on the ground, their strength while unconscious. The regular appearance on the way to school of the man in the gray suit who picked up the mail for Morija, a home for emotionally disturbed men, every morning with his cart. Suddenly he leaves the cart behind, turns about in a circle, throws his hat in the air, zigzags across the street several times with a spastic gait, then continues along his way on the right side of the street, engrossed, as if nothing had happened. Fear, horror, sympathy – none of them feelings that could bring me closer to people.

The so-called healthy were no relief. They allowed no joy or truth to arise, though they often used these words. About the war everyone was stubbornly silent. Injuries were wordlessly treated as God's judgment, a just punishment or just exemption. Those who had been spared were wordlessly despised by those whose lives the war had torn apart. The healthy separated themselves from the wounded, who secretly remained proud of their sacrifice, although this sacrifice did not bring them any kind of prestige. The heroines of everyday life fell into the shadows, women without men. The gap between the cured and the permanently injured could not be bridged. And Sunday confession – "I, poor sinner . . . received and born into sin" – produced only something like a diffuse collective depression; the fact that all of them said it made them all lose credibility for me. Besides, confession obstructed my questions, or led them in a direction which remained completely dark to me.

I felt I didn't belong anywhere. I stayed at home as

much as possible, preferably at the piano in the room where I always sought to be alone, on the piano stool. It was here I was most often to be found outside of school.

Today I got out my old music, somewhat yellow and tattered from much use. In the front, in a backhanded schoolgirl script, is my name. Many notes are written in with my old confirmation pen, which you had to fill with the correct ink; the staff lines are drawn with pencil and ruler: German lieder from the fourteenth through the seventeenth century. I still know all the lyrics by heart; their composers are mostly unknown. "Forget the world and its affairs"; "when they with joy / depart this life / leave this mortal earth"; "whoever can think to put his hope / only in this time / lives a dead life / and dies in sadness."

I love these songs. Tilman Moser calls them and what they elicit "God-poisoning," longing for guidance, care, feeding, watering, gifts. Not I. Perhaps because I acquired them not in a pious God-drunken parish, not forced into the costly bonds of "we," but always alone.

These songs in their loneliness did not become a way for me to communicate with the one to whom they are mostly addressed, namely God. Instead they loop back into a time which is sometimes also my time. Their place is Germany. This is undeniable. Nevertheless what these songs express, what they mean, remains irreconcilable with the content and sound of the word "Germany." If I close my eyes: Germany . . . Speer – spear – helmet – Kohl – cabbage – Walter – Helmut – Victor – victory – *Sieg* – *Heil* – arrow – steel – torture . . . Stop! This corrupted land.

I have tried to hold Germany at bay. My father, the Nazi, loved Germany before all else. He volunteered to go to war for Germany. He hiked on foot from the German

North Sea to the German Alps. He wrote his daughters touching letters from the battlefield about the German birds, deer, and forests, the German countryside and cultural centers, the German soldiers who fed the starving animals and helped the civilian population; lies that concealed mass murder, pillaging, rape, and his own pleasure in these things. My father, a man who remained unknown to me, who got shot in the head outside of Stalingrad. Germany – his land.

Already as a child I thought about where my country was and what the word "homeland" really meant, whether I was missing something if I didn't have one. There was no place to which the word corresponded. I knew no homeland-feeling, and never missed that emotion that's supposed to echo in the hometown bells and sound in the woods of home. I never revisited the places I had lived, never even passed through them again. Nothing was rooted in a place. As for roots in general: I don't want any, don't want to be rooted, don't want to put down roots. I won't have to know the neighbors, talk over garden fences and in stairwells, smell the lilacs once again.

"Everyone needs a homeland," we often hear these days. This poor innocent word should be restored to its rights, after it's been so horribly sullied by German history. This taboo word should be dusted off and should reclaim its holy-metaphysical resonance. We could just as well say "nest" – the need for the homeland-nest, for rest, for continuity and repetition, for merging, for embedding. Many seem to discover their "love for Germany" now that the rockets have brought the truth to light: that these men take war and destruction for granted, and can no longer disguise this with the lie that the condition of war is a regrettable but necessary exception and non-war the normal state, which everyone desires and is striving for. They discover love for this Germany at the very moment when the existence of the means of mass murder has made cheerful deployment on the home front inappropriate – when in fact these weapons have entered so-called public consciousness as machines of ultimate death ready to go off at any moment.

Some years ago, I was traveling home through Italy, which was unbearably hot, in an old VW Beetle, lying on the back seat on the verge of heat stroke. In this semiconscious state these long-suppressed songs – folksongs, sacred music, lieder – surfaced: suddenly "my heart leaps / and cannot be sad / is full of joy and sings / sees only sunshine"; "give up, give up your pains / and bid your cares goodnight"; "The sunshine has gone under / the dark night rushes in"; "Come, sweet death / come, blessed calm"; "The dear sun's light and splendor / has now brought about the day"; "the wheat grows strong / young and old rejoice"; "the raging pent-up sea / rises up with might and urges us swiftly on"; "Arise, my heart, with joy / behold what has happened today"; "the splendor of the earth / must turn to smoke and ash . . ."

The others in the car, an American and a friend with a scrupulously atheistic upbringing, at first tried to ignore my songs. They thought it would end, play itself out. Then they thought I was crazy. What was eerie was that there was no end to it: always new lyrics, new melodies, no repetition. I was in a kind of trance. Each stanza a treasure, a wonderful rediscovery after decades of burial. "If death takes me there / death will be my prize"; "retreat, you mourning spirits"; "rage, world, and crack / I stand here and sing / in such safe calm"; "put an end to all our distress . . ." These songs are my homeland. I carry them with me wherever I am. They are my songs. Hardly anyone knows them. And even if someone else may have heard them, I alone was moved by these deep, sad words and these stirringly simple yet surprising chord changes, this formbound music. Impossible to hear these songs performed by others, recorded or publicly staged, displayed, professionalized. I played and sang them mostly for myself, especially the love songs: "Beautiful love, this song is for you / I wish you goodnight a thousand times"; "Though beams of joy / have melted away / the heart still wants / to bask in their light"; "Away, thoughts / away from me / how can you still torment me so?" And three hundred years earlier: "a woman has managed / through the power of love / to make me desire her / I have no choice / I feel torment / in my innermost heart . . . This I must suffer / and win deceitful death / instead of you." Schubert with his "I'd carve it deep in every tree" is flat by comparison.

The connecting of love and death is the central theme in the love songs, as in the Christian songs. I even forgave the soprano in Bach's *St. Matthew Passion* her Jesus-centeredness; I listened beyond it and heard "To die . . . of love." Love was the realization of love of life, but not a life with less suffering, less wrong, less despair. Utopia was not a better life, now or later, or a more successful love of life: utopia was death, death the end. Death was not cheapened or trivialized, and never banished. "Yes, bitter death / with your anguish / and your retinue / nothing can compare to you."

The connection of life and death, love and death, is comforting in an indescribable way. It is not bitter, not embittered, not disillusioned, not panic-stricken, not miserable. Today there is much talk of our having to "include" death in our thinking, of "dealing with" death. "Weapons philosophy" is supposed to consist in the confrontation with our death. But in reality it consists in the confrontation with the whole naked perfidy of normal human (male) thought and provokes our cold hatred, the cold terror over our heads. So it is not death that is symbolized by the deadly weapon. That's mere talk, intellectual bungling. A life of moderation cannot incorporate death. In these songs death is not brought into life; it is already present, it has already happened, it is already felt, day after day, and not primarily as the consequence of human misdeeds. These songs are comforting because the most terrible event is not being awaited with bated breath; it does not lie ahead, it is already and always here. It is not to be outdone. The intensity of feeling is so explosive that death loses its paralyzing fear.

The irreconcilability remains. The gaping contradiction: there is a place in the "heart" (a metaphor as exhausted as it is irreplaceable), a place in the ear, a space filled with nameless feelings which have remained inexterminable, inexhaustible, repeatable, unconveyable, full of love and, in their intensity, both calm and explosive – and completely devoid of content. And there is the real-life present, which never did become home, in which we never settled down.

These emotions are suspended in an absolutely unknown time, the source of so much love and so much fear about creation and its transitoriness; love of humans in their frailty, of nature in its vulnerability, of the world as it is, whether beautiful or ugly; the feeling that all of creation both has life and loses it. All this next to our shoddy German present, which we cannot love.

Whit-Monday, 1984, 8:15 P.M. "From Russia with Love." For millions of German marks, the broadcasting system has purchased James Bond films and other trash in order to bring them into German living rooms and childrens' rooms in prime time. No big deal. There are much worse films. But on this evening, after consciously and reluctantly sitting through this American abomination – whose leading man, I remember very well, was regarded in the sixties as the epitome of cool, this fondler of weapons and women, accustomed to success, eternally victorious – I was suddenly seized with howling despair. Next came the urge not only to shower and to clean the room but to get this person, along with his friends, male and female, out of the apartment. I often have such a wish. But I also felt helpless terror at the triviality, at the pettiness, of these human specimens now lingering in millions of German rooms and brains, leaving their traces, making impressions, claiming time, brain time. "What's wrong with you today? Aren't you feeling well?" I was asked; there were comforting words and gestures to the effect that perhaps I was overworked, nonsense which pushed my despair even further. A kind of national-hygiene feeling took hold of me: I do not want more and more poison to enter this country. A kind of national compassion. A sudden, overwhelming feeling of "us."

> We're not being forced to stay.
> We're stopping. Let's end the routine.
> Or the end is going to be spoiled too.[1]

The maintenance of the corporate "body" of a people whose stupidity is probably incurable is not in and of itself a worthy goal; its continued existence cannot be the measure of all interests. There are downfalls that are not regrettable.

What's left is farewell. "Feelings about the state of the nation" are feelings of farewell: the recognition that this people, this country, is coming to an end, has come to an end.

It is not just the acts which invented and shaped the form of this Germany that are hateful and deserve to perish – not just this poisoned, diluted, paltry image, this product of neglect, the thoughts and feelings of the male rulers and their non-ruling allies in this country, the image evoked by Germany's broadcasters, who depict whatever they deem worthy of preservation and representation – an image which levels, smooths over, and conceals everything alive, chaotic, incomprehensible, everything not known, not understood, everything unique or even unusual, everything incalculable and unpredictable. How could we love such a mirror?

But this country is more than an image, designed from on high, a creation of consciousness. What such a narrow and nasty construction perpetually brings forth is the domesticated and uniform "German" species.

This creature facing his downfall is not happy, not healthy, not free, not good, not creative. These women are not strong, not loving, not inventive, not generous, not present, not supportive. They gnaw at themselves, they direct their dissatisfaction with life against themselves and each other. They direct their shrunken desire toward the male body, shabby or obese as it is, and to the male mind, which, though bankrupt, is still full of itself.

Should there still exist remnants of loving feelings, outbreaks of affection for this land, this nation, its brutal history and present and its contradictory culture, they should be expressed not through negation alone, but through a melancholy feeling of separation.

6

FEMINISM
AND MORALITY

The decade of the eighties, like scarcely any other time before it, served to bring about the collapse of all remaining illusions about the future of this earth and of these human beings, male and female. The prevailing immorality which surrounds us and in which we participate is no academic problem – it's become a problem of survival. And so today it's not a question of the search for new images of a new ideal being, nor of the intention every morality has to bring the empirical human being closer to an ideal. It's a question of preventing the self-liquidation of humankind – or at least, more modestly, of the conclusions we want to draw from the fact that this self-liquidation is now possible. This possibility has been expedited, if not caused, by the white man's assumption that, by abolishing the symbol of a superior God, he can recoup what was projected onto it, namely a part of his male being, and so acquire unforeseen powers of subordination and mastery over nature, impoverished countries, and women. It has become apparent, however, that these hoped-for qualities are not at men's disposal.

We are living in a historically exceptional situation – extraordinary, unique, and unprecedented. This uniqueness does not lie in the fact that the present, with its monstrous and malignant realities, has subjected us to something qualitatively new. What's unique is that now everyone has the opportunity to recognize the malignancy of reality – of the people who create it, assist in its creation, or put up with it. Even the most minimal of myths, which have always arisen as open or secret hopes – above all the myth of "not yet" – are buried. The facts which are sent into every living room, into every brain, must disrupt and destroy all the habits of repression at their core. We can see, even without the curse or the blessing of prophetic gifts. Inhabitants of the Western world are resolutely spreading their deadly disease, sowing it far and wide, practicing at great expense the art of killing and destroying, and granting carte blanche to the government engineers who organize it all. In light of the present facts the moral foundations of patriarchal civilization lie in ruins; they have become unhinged.

The present historical situation is characterized by the devaluation of Western man. However self-evident it may appear, this is a dramatic claim. Man as the bearer and determiner of value in patriarchal culture is being unveiled – through his harmful, careless, or stupid acts – as the past and present cause of danger to life, to humanity, to the earth. Man as the bearer of culture is not to be trusted, not to be believed; no hopes can be set on him, no future associated with him. What he has thought and done, what he has brought into the world and what he has allowed to happen – that is, what he has made into history, into reality – is useless as orientation in the thicket of "good" and "evil," and has forfeited its value. Whatever used to be considered valuable, right, important, true, reasonable, justifiable, or exemplary, no longer is. The value of what man used to value has been exposed as delusion.

The masculine has in this culture been the bearer and determiner of value. Accordingly, the basic requirement of a patriarchal female morality is that it perform mystifications that heighten male value and at the same time reduce female value. If man as the bearer of value is no longer of sound mind, no longer credible, he becomes incompetent as the determiner of value as well.

Now, what happens to women if they are no longer willing to accept man as the bearer and determiner of value, if they try first of all not to value what patriarchal man himself embodied socially as value? If they are not willing to see their own value as defined by man, from his male point of view? And if they do not value, at least not uncritically, what man values in the world?

Women fall into a void. This does not mean that they were previously on solid ground. For man as the determiner of value requires women to maintain empty ego-spaces in readiness for him to fill. These empty ego-spaces, in keeping with a patriarchal female morality, are fulfilled by being filled full with him.[1] The worthiness of the male and the worthlessness of the female are bound up with the woman's readiness to be empty, to prepare her "dwelling" for man; being fulfilled by a man, through him, requires her to reserve a space for him to inhabit, give content to, illustrate.

The devaluation and demystification of man does not mean that this empty space is now at woman's disposal, ready to be newly furnished, a beckoning new territory. No – it is bare and uncultivated, without models or concepts, without images or myths. Truly to perceive and endure this is, as I see it, the decisive challenge for feminists in the present situation.

We cannot simply say: Patriarchy has turned out to be a form of society whose predominant members, men, saw as valuable something that turned out not to be valuable. Therefore we women are finally taking our different morality out of the closet, setting the priorities ourselves, replacing and occupying the empty spaces. I see this fine challenge as an ahistorical illusion. We are not bounding into unoccupied territory; such territory doesn't exist. Besides, we have nothing in our possession, or not enough, with which to occupy this no place in our own way – a completely different, brand-new way.

The moral bankruptcy of Western man undermines this supposedly very different female morality. It is not self-sufficient; it is dependent, amalgamated. It has developed during this same polluted history as a morality of service to man, as a morality of relationship, whose assumptions stand and fall with the acceptance of the disparity between the sexes – of the male claim to superiority, to being worthy of support and protection, and thus to special social and personal importance. The female moral repertoire is devalued along with the devaluation of man as the bearer of morals.

This leaves women in a moral vacuum. Their actual or imagined relationships with man or with maleness have lost their significance. The entire ideological structure breaks down if those who created it and upheld it disqualify themselves. Their standards and ideas, their arguments, become irrelevant. The ideological and material authority figure – the emotional, sexual, and intellectual center of reference – has become a moral phantom, laughable and deeply embarrassing.

Likewise with the woman, as long as she prefers to go on letting herself be determined by this phantom and letting herself be labeled by his seal, his approval, his gaze.

Women's historical crimes are to be found in their unquestioning support or ingenuous approval of male actions and decisions, in their dependable confirmation and zealous covering up, in their forcibly ignoring and averting their own gaze, in their forcible repression of their own judgment. The crime of women was not the abolition of God, but the affirmation of the ersatz male version of him. Women topped off this great male feat by adding to their earlier devotion to God devotion to mortal man. Women's guilt consists not in overrating themselves, but in directly or indirectly accepting the men who overrate themselves.

Now, the exposure of the male does not come about naturally and of its own accord; it can happen only as an act of women. And this exposure is not simply an intellectual or deliberate act. On the one hand, the world before us is stripped utterly bare, its people unclothed; we don't need to clear away pretty scenery in order to recognize the violent and pitiable figure of Western man. But the unvarnished reality is obviously scarcely bearable. To have its naked vileness constantly before our eyes – to experience its moral insufficency simultaneously with its supreme material power – confronts women with a void that demonstrates how little space is available for thinking and living independent of man as a reference point.

Man was and is the orientation of most women, their life content, the focus of their care and their senses, standard and guide – not only in bed, but in the mind, in life plans, in the economy of feelings. To empty this central space, to catapult the male out of it, to give up one's contradictory security in the idealized male figure threatens us with chaotic disorientation, an inferno of insecurity over how women might be and what we might do.

The moral obliteration of God's little stand-in is bound to have unforeseeable and problematic consequences for the birth of a feminist morality.

A parallel comes to mind: another instance of devaluation in our culture, which in the course of the Enlightenment under the formula "God is dead" initiated the abolition of the old divine superego by the male and for the male. The analogy between the devaluation of God by man and the devaluation of man by woman, however, lies not in the historical parallels but in the historical differences, which make us aware of the incomparability of the process in which women find themselves today.

Friedrich Nietzsche described the increasing irrelevance of Western Christian morality and self-idolization with a parable.

> Have you not heard of that madman who lit a lantern in the bright morning hours, ran to the market place, and cried incessantly: "I seek God! I seek God!" . . . "Whither is God?" he cried; "I will tell you. *We have killed him* – you and I. All of us are his murderers. But how did we do this? . . . What were we doing when we unchained this earth from its sun? Whither is it moving now? Whither are we moving? . . . Are we

not plunging continually? . . . Are we not straying as
through an infinite nothing? . . . Is not the greatness
of this deed too great for us? Must we ourselves not
become gods simply to appear worthy of it? There
has never been a greater deed; and whoever is born
after us – for the sake of this deed he will belong to a
higher history than all history hitherto.[2]

The devaluation of God brought forth contradictions:
the elevation of self and an expectation of upward evolution
of people and culture, and at the same time the surrender of
the self and an expectation of final decline and degeneration
of civilized people. Thus on the one hand it resulted in a
great revitalization, a kind of compensation for the loss of
God; a great upheaval, understood as a symptom of a "higher
power"; a movement directly into the heart of life, unconditionally expansive and extravagant; an intention to pave
the way for a free and lawless society and to approve the
extermination of the old one as an act of necessary hygiene.
But on the other hand it produced an overtaxing of the self,
that is, both need for and denial of the godly ideal; the vision
of one's own male sex in its hour of death, of one's own
decline, albeit as adventurous, dangerous, appealing as ever
– of aesthetic self-sacrifice; sometimes great disgust and
insight into the absurdity of vanity. It meant bidding farewell
to the fantasy that the human male, with his great and noble
future, is the purpose of world history; it meant seeing that
he might just as well lead downward as upward, and that
this planet earth along with the human race is nothing but
an indeterminate animal which happens to be equipped with
an interesting but uncontrolled intelligence.

Between the two dramas of devaluation – the end of God as moral authority, as determined by the enlightened man, and the end of contemporary man as moral authority, as discerned by any woman with her eyes open – the following vast differences can be seen:

1.   The devaluation of God by man was a matter of faith. The devaluation of man today is a historical fact. Neither the existence nor the death of God could be proved, but any woman can easily observe the moral abdication of the male. The facts unambiguously show that what has brought the earth to its present state is not supernatural or natural forces. We don't need the nit-picking interpretations of a few man-hating women in order to see the devastations and the devastators. The facts can't be doctored; they won't allow us to conceal them or shift them onto anyone but the real perpetrators.

2.   The devaluation of God by man was synonymous with the overthrow of God. The devaluation of man by woman is synonymous with his exposure. The abdication of Western man is an act of consciousness and recognition on the part of women. It does not effect itself and is not effected by everyone. Neither man's physical survival nor his position of power in the moral slums of politics, business, and social institutions is in jeopardy; men's systematic mutual support constantly safeguards them. For this reason it is still possible to uphold the illusion of man's quality and of our relationship to him and to adapt our senses to this illusion.

3.   The devaluation of God by man was an active deed of men; they saw to it that God was dead. The devaluation of

man is no active deed of women, no act of abolition, but something that's already happened which women are now confronting. Women did not arrange a massacre – man simply shrank and collapsed. True, women contributed to the slow decay by supporting men in overrating themselves; they joined in the moral suicide by a shared overrating of the male. Women suffered a great deal from this, but they also tried to use it to raise their own status a little. In constructing and caring for the male pedestal and installing themselves on the footstool beneath it, they made certain that the over-praising and mystification of the male was their handiwork as well.

4.   The devaluation of God by man happened because men wanted to free themselves from a moral dictatorship, not because God had behaved immorally. The devaluation of man, on the other hand, happens because men have failed morally. When God was abolished there was no factual proof that He had done anything wrong. If the world was experi-enced as a vale of tears where people could not spend their lives in pure happiness, still there was no certainty that God was responsible. Today, on the other hand, the evidence can be established with certainty. It culminates in the mania of research that violates all boundaries, foremost in the destruc-tion of two nuclei, the atomic nucleus and the cell nucleus, and in the fact that man, instead of putting a stop to these acts of destruction, developed them into gigantic economic and political enterprises.

5.   The devaluation of God by man was connected with the male will to recapture the divine powers he had assigned to the deity. The devaluation of man by woman, in contrast,

does not spring from the impulse to assimilate male powers, for these powers are not worthy of assimilation and aspiration. Women have taken upon themselves the act of self-impoverishment. But it's not as if something richer could have been demanded from men. God was thought of as male, and men tried to be like Him. But now it's not a question of women wanting to be representative, like an ideal male self – it's a question of radical detachment from the relations of complementarity, confirmation, and corruptibility. Women are withdrawing without pocketing what they would like to take with them.

6.   The devaluation of God succeeded because men were convinced of the infallibility of their own intellect and because the male desire for knowledge felt badly thwarted by the institution of God. The devaluation of man, in contrast, is not triggered by an ever-expanding and long-restrained hunger for knowledge in women. Such a hunger is not what drives women to a renewed attempt to learn what holds this world together and to construct knowledge differently, on their own, in a new and better way. Their insight, compelled by observation, their forced knowledge of the moral death of man, frightens women more than it frees them.

7.   The devaluation of God was understood by men as a major feat, as humanity's greatest hour, as the very act of liberation which exalted humanity. They envisioned new horizons, without borders or customs duties. They envisioned a new dawn. The devaluation of man by woman, in contrast, cannot be a thrilling feat of liberation because men still hold the actual power in their hands, even after their moral demise. Women do not face an open ocean, an unlimited horizon.

Everything is preordained and already occupied, filled with Hiroshima a million times over.

8.   The devaluation of God by man was bound up with the hope that men could replace the previously divine ideals, truths, and comforts with empirical knowledge. It was not that morality was being abolished, but that the bearer of morality was being replaced. The devaluation of man by woman, in contrast, is not bound up with the expectation that a replacement is to be found in themselves, that they already possess these valuable powers and simply have to deploy them at last. It is not a question of ousting the male through identification, but of detaching, of turning away, without attempting to substitute anything.

9.   The devaluation of God by man led men to wandering as a form of existence. The devaluation of men by women does not lead to journeying guided by great curiosity. Seeking out the strange and questionable in life does not have the attraction of the new or the forbidden. The ease of wandering and roving depends on the existence of paths where surprising things can be found. But the paths are already well worn, thoroughly explored, and paved, marked and labeled. There is no escape in moving forward, since there is no unexplored direction.

10.   The devaluation of God by man was connected with the refusal to be self-critical and to question one's own actions. The devaluation of man by woman is further tied to a division of labor: women are taking on the task of recognizing and naming artifices, facades, and deceptions. Women both critique themselves and critique men on their behalf.

This division of labor is a symptom of male moral decay; otherwise men would have taken this work on themselves.

11. The devaluation of God by man exposed men to the fear that now they would really have to take over and control everything, so as not in the end to be crushed by the power they had disenthroned or to run up against their own limits. The devaluation of man by woman, in contrast, is not bound up with the fear that she now has to take the wheel and demonstrate her qualification for leadership. Woman's fear must continue to be focused on male deeds and male agents and on her own insufficiencies. The idea of being able to do everything is one that women, realistically enough, never developed in the first place.

12. The devaluation of God was no stroke of retribution by man and was not followed by retribution against God. For God didn't really exist and couldn't really do anything. In fact, He hadn't really robbed man of anything. Instead, men had – as they saw it – deprived themselves in the service of a delusion. They could at best avenge themselves on their own kind, those who had seduced them to the deception, on the church and the authorities. The devaluation of man by woman, in contrast, could pave the way for getting even. Women are surrounded by opportunities of revenge for what man has done and continues to do; he's easy to catch in the act. The perpetrators have been identified. Yet there is no authority holding them to account. They may be observed but they go on about their business. They have an address, a telephone number. They are accessible. But they know that they can't be turned in.

These points make it clear that men's moral bankruptcy is not the result of an active decision, a creative deed by women; that women are not now entering their own time in which they can set the standards; that women have before them not an open field where they can cultivate afresh and experiment anew, but rather a prefabricated, contaminated earth.

Women do not embark upon the project of devaluation devoid of history, unabused and unburdened. Indeed, it confronts us with our history, with our entire contradictory repertoire of questionable valuations and dissolving values. This history is contradictory. It is the history of female slaves with their slave morality; of female collaborators with their morality of complicity; of housewives with their housewife morality; of resisters with their resistance morality; of sufferers with their morality of suffering. And the contradictions of these moralities explain something of the difficulty women have today in negotiating within the illegal and the legal, the public and the secret acts of the present, marked by cynical matter-of-factness and criminal normalcy.

Women's moral history is a splintered one. The history of female slaves is divided between deadly hatred, revenge, and maidenly devotion to the master; the history of female complicity between the betrayal of women and the individual's learning process; the history of housewives between being protected by men and tied down by them; the history of emancipation and resistance between simultaneous approach to and avoidance of men; the history of the sick between suffering and knowing, a history which contains incentives to life, love, and sympathy – as well as to capitulation.

Such a history has not exactly been able to teach women consistency. Its legacies are the constant duality of female experience, the constantly lurking double-binds in which all paths can lead to failure, the eternal ambivalence. Yet its currency is beginning to come to an end for every woman who is willing to remove herself, to separate herself radically from the indecisiveness of her previous history. Consistency with our present experience can be introduced without any great feminist fanfare. It doesn't lead to easy answers, either: our time is without precedent, without parallel, without predecessors, and moreover without presentiment. We are not inspired by great daring, the joy of acting, the thirst for change. In spite of this the mood, the air, and the light have changed. As so often before, women are now being thrown back upon themselves – upon the insecure, riven creatures that we are, without crutches or stays. What's noteworthy here is only this: we do not want to redesign this world yet again as a willed act of creation – not for anything. Useful to this end would be to think rigorous and simple thoughts, soberly and unsentimentally, and to overcome the intimidation of our intelligence. Women have not had much experience with the truth. Now is the measure of how much truth we can bear.

7

THE TURNING POINT: TURNING AWAY?

P erceiving the extent of our species' capacity for destruction is bound to open up mental escape routes into any credo that relieves us of the malignant facts of the present. Hence the reassurances that have come along of late: the consolations, distractions, and trivializations disguised as scientific prognoses about our future.

Prophets and prophetesses have recently and hastily sprung up to tell of the approach of a new age, of a turning point, of the great transformation on its way. The notion of people's actual misery can obviously be borne only for a moment, or at least we'll do anything so as not to have to bear it for any longer. People are once again compelled to conjure up future prospects, intellectual rest-stations, the spirit of a new Advent. Or else they're driven to the devout quest for unambiguous explanations and behavioral directives, for strategies for arriving at solutions, faith, goals, perspectives – for a way of rethinking that succeeds in turning our thoughts away.

There also appear in these unholy and unhealthy times professors of forgetting, who prevent us from thinking and feeling things through to the end. In the market place of new worldviews the demand is especially strong for those items which work against the general confusion, so that no fear, no hatred, no despair is unleashed: prescriptions against humanity's self-inflicted terminal disease, comforters of the terminally ill. Without fail, they clear away everything that seems pointless, hopeless, or ambiguous.[1]

Reading these "transformational thinkers" – both male and female – put me in the worst physical and mental condition: my utter inability to digest this fare brought on stomach ache, the feeling of having overeaten, loss of appetite, foul mood, complete aversion to taking in even one more word – a constipation of the mind with every accumulating sentence, a standstill of ideas and curiosity of every sort. Especially annoying was that this material couldn't immediately be evacuated. It weighed me down to the point of paralysis and sat sluggishly and impudently in my head and entrails. Brain pollution, poison for women. A repulsive "spirit of reconciliation," an invitation to consensus and fusion that assumes the garb of science and wise prophecy with a great all-embracing gesture of acceptance.

The new literature on this "transformation" claims without any doubt that a great change of reality *is* taking place, that a fundamental shift in consciousness has already swept over humanity like an avalanche. Once we have made the requisite journey inward and finally achieved global planetary consciousness, "then the way to a solution, that is, overcoming the world crises out there, will come about on its own."[2] Don't panic, keep calm and look forward to meaningful solutions.

The American journalist Marilyn Ferguson's book *The*

Aquarian Conspiracy: Transformation in the Age of Aquarius sold a
quarter of a million copies in the United States within a few
months, has been translated into French, German, Dutch,
Swedish, Japanese, and Esperanto, and has won the hearts of
German feminists as well. The author radiates an absolutely
manic, hypermanic, Ameri-manic euphoria of change. She
sees the "breakthrough," the social transformation, emerging
everywhere. Already affected are "medicine, education, the
social sciences and government" (p. 18). The conspiracy
reaches across all social and intellectual strata: teachers,
bureaucrats, famous scientists, government officials, lawmak-
ers, artists, millionaires, taxi drivers, celebrities, leaders of
medicine, education, law, psychology . . . Everything is possible; you just have to want to progress and free yourself of
old ideas. The perspective of the "new lights" will win out.[3]
Let's make the "intuitive leap" into the collective paradigm
shift. The gift of insight is open to everyone and we are not
limited by any conditioning.[4]

Marilyn Ferguson frankly reports that top business
managers have proven a receptive audience for her book –
that is, people who appreciate novelty, who are used to
thinking flexibly, pragmatically, and in a results-oriented way
and who take an immediate interest in anything that works
(p. 72). In an interview with *New Age Magazine,* the author
explains the success of her book, saying it's a mirror for
people who see themselves at a dead end, as their customary
interpretation of the world no longer fits and no new pattern
of interpretation has emerged. Ferguson compares this situation in its desperate perplexity to Linus (from *Peanuts*) when
his security blanket happens to be in the dryer, or to a
detective who thought he understood the context of a crime,

but finds more and more inconsistencies which finally force him to drop his version of the case in favor of one which better corresponds to the new information.

Both images strike me as misleading and careless. For one thing, Linus gets his old security blanket back when it's washed and dry and then everything is as good as new. For another, the world has not been in good shape (with or without security blankets) as long as people's images of the world have agreed with what they wanted to see. For the detective, moreover, there *is* in the end a concrete solution to the tangled proceedings – he simply has to find it. Every reasonable person can see that a wrong solution is wrong, that it has to be replaced by the correct one, and that to clear up the case one must, as quickly as possible, get on the trail of the one correct solution. But the situation of humanity, of women and men, can't be solved like a math problem or a criminal case. And even if it could be, the right solution would never be in the interest of all parties. The criminal and his confederates are hardly interested in having the case explained and correctly solved. And sometimes certainly we would rather see the criminals at large than their pursuers, and we wish on the pursuers all the mistakes in the world. In any case, I believe that anyone who proclaims that there now exists a universal solution is a con artist, a charlatan, a liar, or simply a dope. The example of Ferguson demonstrates the current level of nonsense in this "transformation" business. Her example, unfortunately, is not unique. Today it is enough to assure everyone "it'll be all right. See, it is all right! People are better than they seemed a while ago, and you too, you're OK, I'm OK, and besides: just imagine, a gentle but unstoppable quiet revolution is taking place and you are part of it! And you women, you especially, for very essential elements of this change come from the feminist idea bank. Men are now finally beginning to incorporate these into their worldview. We can breathe a sigh of relief. We have no good reason to see men as enemies anymore. After all, we really all want the same thing, women and men, feminists and gentlemen! . . ." And so they all agree with a sigh of relief, seeing the great unifying transformation extending all the way from the family to the offices of the ministers of war.

The willingness to trust in the promise of positive change seems limitless; not so the desire to analyze it. Only the result, the directive, counts and is heard. It is simply clear that something positive must result. Everything else was a temporary, understandable low. There is a widespread willingness to be calmed and cheered, a willingness to make the anthropological-political catastrophe manageable by transforming it into a psychological one; to count ourselves among the "conspirators" – invisible and inconspicuous though they are.[5] And of course along with this everyone needs a smattering of knowledge about Zen, Tao, and I Ching, and theoretical physics, to know a few tokens of the Far East and naturally to strive for overall de-Westernization.[6] A perpetually ineffectual smattering.

In the literature of "transformation" we encounter lists of the "parameters" of a desired society which we can approach by making changes, by developing . . . dismantling . . . building up . . .[7] An infusion of some Marx (operative word, "society"), some Freud (operative word, "repression"), some Reich (operative word, "liberated sexuality"), actualized, fertilized with some Gandhi (operative word, "nonviolence," discreetly ignoring the equally possible operative word "asceticism"), some Bateson (operative words, "ecology" and "nature and spirit"), some feminism (operative words, "biological principle of gentle strength"), some spirituality (operative word, "holism"). This potpourri is stirred up with a trendy vocabulary: network, merging, interdependence, complexity, pulsation, oscillation, energy, integration, and of course paradigm shift. Repressive morality, according to the analysis of the Now, constrains human potential; the repressed life force has to find an emergency outlet and so necessarily takes on a violent, destructive form. As if the tiniest bit of trust in the quality of this "human," "natural" potential were justified – in a "universal love" issuing from biological sources![8] You only need to look at the war reports of men such as Ernst Jünger to see how their potential was unleashed as a sexualized lust for murder.[9]

Haste in the search for easy answers leads to further flowerings of this kind. The British economist Hazel Henderson, who lives in the United States (she was one of the ghostwriters for Fritjof Capra, the star author of the "turning point"), recommends tuning in to our primitive programming, which is older than our cultural programming, and tuning in to "Nature, our surest teacher." And women should simply reclaim the reproductive rights biology has given them. "All that women would need to do to create a quiet revolution is to resume the old practice of keeping the paternity of their children a secret."[10]

Back, in other words, to the practices and the level of knowledge of prepatriarchal societies, in which women were revered thanks to the fact that they could grow human life in their bodies, without men knowing in the least that they too participated in this process in a rather simple and pleasant manner. Back, then, to the time before attempts at scientific thought, when cause and effect could not yet be perceived or explored; back to the magical animistic divinings of cultures attuned to fertility and seasonal cycles.

This new thinking, the new "planetary agenda" (Henderson), is now groping hungrily for substance, and parts of the women's movement, in their search for identity and history, have turned in its direction – on a trial basis, so to speak, and dubiously enough. There's hardly a New Age author who resists making the comment (important to him) that the "feminist consciousness which arose from the women's movement" is what will profoundly alter the old system. Such remarks are to be found for the most part in explanatory sections, in the introductions or in the crescendo of concluding phrases.[11] Here it's clearly stated that the bearer of this development is not women but the feminist or feminine consciousness, the "realization of female principles," or the "*yin* perspective," which will "push out the boundaries of the old *yang* paradigm" and to which men will increasingly open themselves.[12] "Ecofeminism" involves the resacralization of nature, the magic of life, occult laws, magic circles, cycles, vibrations, rhythms, fertility, moon-worship, natural connection with the spirit of the earth goddess Gaia, and the wonderful embracing of . . . pain, of entropy, of life and death, of coming and going, up and away.[13] And very soon we will see the merging of ecofeminism and ecophilosophy, whose new knowledge at this moment still flows in a neighboring riverbed. But a tentative pairing of experience (female, ecofeminism) with knowledge (male, ecophilosophy), of woman's Gaia-bound natural intuition with men's exceptionally rich sum total of ecological knowledge, will take place with the aim of ending and overcoming Cartesian modes of thought and discourse once and for all.

Soon we'll all be in the same riverbed! The synthesis of ecofeminism and ecophilosophy, the leveling of the riverbed for our collective movement, is being managed by enlightened men who will embrace the female principle and the energies flowing from it and bring it to maturity in themselves.[14] The "turning point" is therefore supposed to mark a return to the "feminine or intuitive aspect" of nature; yang is retreating – yang, not men.[15] A principle of nature is shifting and fluctuating; the present time has the honor of witnessing the inevitable reappropriation of a holistic-ecological-feminine value system by men. And so the women's movement is recognized as the greatest innovative power of the eighties and nineties, a precisely limited span of time during which women may once again bring their healing higher morality into the patriarchal world. All of this is happening thanks to the capacity, "inherent to female brains," to see the whole and to produce a "more deeply sustaining relationship to the universe." Women can eliminate men's false ideas of their own perfection since they are "neurologically" more flexible and are "more intuitive, sensitive and feeling."[16] *Women can remain as they are.*

I consider all this to be worthless trash, at least in synopsis. (Even if Capra, for example, has doubtless done a good job of pulling together certain scientific developments, especially for lay people, his arguments don't add up. The glaring contradictions between the revolutionary discoveries of the-oretical physics and their realization in atomic weapons, the

contradiction between woman's wonderful nature and her
social situation do not enter his – or any of the others' –
field of vision.) And it is women, unfortunately, who seem
to have been especially receptive to the promises and reassurances of this trash.

Various phenomena of the times are adduced and interpreted
as evidence of a gentle revolutionary force – gentle because
it is embedded in consciousness, as Götterdämmerung, as
the breakthrough of planetary culture, as the dawn of the
"solar age."[17] With the collapse of the old – mechanistic –
worldview of the West and its reductionistic credo, the new
will arise in the rhythm of natural movement; this is stated
in the *I Ching,* Hexagram 24: *Fiu.*[18] As soon as leaders of
opinion, the shamans of modernity, begin to use the new
paradigm, it will unnoticeably but rapidly become "the carpet
upon which the majority stands."[19] All emigrants to the inner
world, all Western capitalists, all friends of the body and the
earth, all bioenergeticists, joggers, yoga gymnasts, enthusiasts
of psychoaerobics, psychonautics, and LSD therapy, all alternative tourists, dolphin and interspecies communicants, all
peace activists, environmentalists, and soft technologists, all
of *them,* all of *us,* the women's movement, the spiritual
movement, the self-actualization movement, the therapy
movement, the health movement; all are participants in the
conspiratorial counterculture and all are linked – at least in
orientation – by the ecological ethic they have in common.

It is always processes of *consciousness,* scientific and cultural
trends, that will cause the disaster to melt away.[20] To *see* the

universe as a harmonious indivisible whole is the "lightning for a fire."[21] If we want to achieve the natural condition of "ecological planetarism" (Capra) we need no social critique; we need only to lay down our blinders, to jettison useless thinking, to admit a new perception of reality.

This new consciousness contains the guarantee of the correct and desired effect, of the saving political consequence. I doubt if such changes in consciousness within existing power relationships are fundamentally different in quality or probability of success than the transformations that have taken place over and over with varying degrees of clarity and severity in all patriarchal, capitalist, or socialist societies – on the part of rulers, with the practical aim of adapting political decisions to changing economic and ideological conditions, and on the part of individuals or groups of people, with the aim of withdrawing from the mainstream of prevailing views or of denying the government control of their thoughts. Overestimating the political effectiveness of such deviations in consciousness proves nothing other than total ignorance of actual power relationships and the current facts, which exist *materially,* and not simply as false perception – even if the world should turn out to be merely "sound" and even if the atom is vibration instead of matter.

The supposedly unstoppable world order that is breaking through with new ecological rules of play is not grounded in anything like moral insights or conscious choices by men and women, rulers and ruled; thus it is not based on a rupture with, separation from, the structures of violence, injustice, subordination, and conformity. The new world order, the foundation for ecological interconnectedness, is *coming about* scientifically and no doubt sensibly for everyone, demonstrably so. The change is being introduced by way of scientific discoveries and is gaining in tempo, according to Capra. This way of thinking is in agreement with the views of Eastern cultures, especially of Taoism, and especially with the theories of "modern" physics.[22] So no one is harmed in any way. Nothing more has to be decided, judged, refused, or undertaken at one's own moral risk, at the risk of transgression, limitation, discrimination, or loneliness. *It is coming about.* What a gentle solution, what a smooth, conflict-free solution!

The knowledge that living systems can regulate themselves without sinking into chaos and entropy, as long as the human male does not intervene in a directing, planning, manipulating way, would doubtless be the main hope of deliverance for patriarchal man, that is, for the male in patriarchy. Such thinking prohibits the claim of supremacy in relation to nature, the conceit that one is made of better "stuff," and so it forbids a hierarchy of value between humans on the one hand and all other living creatures on the other. It is an emergency brake for men playing God, urging them in the direction of humility and modesty and away from historical megalomania, a prohibition of access and intervention, a prohibition of destruction and all imperialist and touristic conquests. Yet even apart from the fact that these are all *moral* requirements, which demand individual decision making, restraint, self-control — apart from that, this is not sufficient, at least not for women. In a rampant politicization of the concept of ecology, the distinction between humans and between women and men in patriarchies also evaporates. This prohibits our intervention as well, our criticism of and our rage at the existing systems in which we have to live; it prohibits us from judging, from making discriminations. It means renouncing a faculty apparently given only to human beings – namely, the capacity to act and think morally, which means having to choose constantly from among a large number of possibilities. We cannot act as if we were just like daisies or butterflies in an ecosystem or like worms in a puddle. In ecosystem thought our "morality" would consist entirely in respecting and not harming holistic ecological principles. Self-regulating systems in the image of nature are not to be criticized; at most they are just to be understood. They possess their own spirit, their own dynamic. Any critique as well as any active disturbance and devaluing of such systems would be profoundly unecological – a violation of the natural laws in their eternal wisdom. This way of thinking rules out the struggle against injustice and all recognizable atrocities. It pacifies the relationship between men and women. It makes a phony ecological peace.

So let's all stay put. Let's agree there are no enemies and supporters, followers and deviants, since all oppositions, "good" and "evil," are abolished in the great ecosystem of which we are part.[23] Let us embrace the motto that a Tibetan monk recently proclaimed at the dance of the lamas in a Himalayan monastery, to the restrained applause of a New Age audience from Berlin: "We like everything! We love everybody!" Let us go on ecologizing, nestled in the spirit of Gaia, integrated into the spiritual system of the planets that in turn participates in a universal cosmic spirit.

The problematic of extending an ecological concept into a "worldview" intensifies when social systems, ways of life historically produced by humans, are to be treated like ecosystems. In the order of nature, the individual human spiritual system is embedded in the spirit of social, biological, planetary systems; all of them "partake somehow of the universal or cosmic spirit."[24] This spirit could be called God, the spirit of the universe, the self-regulating dynamic of the entire cosmos.

This honorable intellectual construct, which in the face of our destructive present has proved more fascinating than ever before, and precisely to the criminals of the West and their female accomplices, does *not* as I see it explain the relationship of human to nature to cosmos – botched, contradictory, and hostile since human creation – or the relations between human beings and between the sexes. Like all monomaniacal attempts at universal explanation, it is in need of demystification. It does not withstand the temptation to construct, out of the latest political redefinition of the relationships between man and nature and between human and nonhuman, an all-embracing model of human existence drawn from biology or physics. Shortsighted (yet all too far-seeing) and immodest, like their mechanistic predecessors, the New Age authors try again to search for the building block, the fundamental principle, the universal formula that's common to all animate and inanimate things – try, for example, to draw from the observation of subatomic phenomena inferences about human relations and consciousness.[25] Again they think they're on to the secret of creation, without paying attention to what's really wrong with actual living and suffering human beings.

Systems thinking, whether applied to the human individual, to societies, or to ecosystems – this approach to present society – is as disastrous as it is absurd in light of central cybernetic and systems-theory concepts like self-regulation, adaptation, and homeostasis. Biological organisms or systems have the tendency to organize themselves, to regenerate, to acclimate, in order to achieve a condition of steady state. They are conservative in the sense that they can balance out disturbances by flexibly adapting to changing inner or outer conditions so as not to endanger their system, their mutual network. They are homeostatic inasmuch as the constancy of any variable is upheld by the reversible or permanent change of other variables. In principle the point is always to prevent complete destruction of the system. This adaptability to a basic design of nature was seen in evolution theory as fundamentally beneficial from the point of view of preservation of the species. Today everyone knows that such adaptations and changes can be just as catastrophic as they are beneficial, not only within human-made systems but also in nature without human intervention.[26] Adaptation and flexibility do not necessarily guarantee the survival or refinement of the species. We cannot trust that our capacities are on a natural evolutionary path – albeit a crooked one – toward ever more creative uses for one and all. Evolution does not simply lay out a wonderful plan for creation; instead, it proves as ugly as it is beautiful, both ingenious and pathological, creative and self-destructive.

The theoretical equation of self-regulating biological systems with social "systems," such as the family, is a scientific and political scandal. All of the authors I've mentioned implicitly treat male and female, human families and societies, with their totally rotten and immoral structure and history, as nature pure and simple, as systems which function according to ecological principles – except when they're occasionally attacked by "system diseases" (Bateson) in which the network slips out of control. The quality of these systems is shown by their capacity to maintain homeostasis through disturbances and irritations. *Homeostasis despite* . . .

This is precisely woman's historical achievement – and failure. This is domestic peace. Within the family, who regulates adaptation to difficult conditions; who muffles "disturbances" like outbreaks of male violence, women asking too much, asking too little, failing to ask, the social environment's deforming influences on children and others, unpaid work, injustices, hierarchies? Who regulates this system and is supposed to go on regulating it by any and all means? The female. It's not "the system" that somehow does the regulating, but the absurd, self-destructive subordination and over-exertion of the female, in the interest of maintaining the family system. For the male the system achieves balance or homeostasis if the woman passively or actively accepts the sexual hierarchy, if she resourcefully and inconspicuously contributes to it. Or if she complies with the male's narcissistic ideal by helping him to overcome his imperfection, by nourishing him with her long-prized femininity – woman's ancient task, her "integrative power."[27]

Women are being talked into a conciliatory, unifying or reunifying worldview, which with great skill sabotages all their attempts to free themselves from their collective, which is to say reciprocal, arrangement with men. It renews their monopolization and occupation, renews the engagement and the stranglehold, using gentle energy instead of force. And this at a stage of patriarchy when women have been shown and have begun to see the demoralization of the patriarchal male perhaps more clearly than ever before; when women no longer view as their only possibility in life the company and camaraderie of men, or the gift of a child, or sacrificing to a man. The reconciliation is to be effected and celebrated according to men's plans and criteria. But at the same time it cannot be a sham reconciliation. This reconciliation will not take place in any simple, pretty way, not after the thousands of years of war against women, not after the basic time-honored formula of valorizing women's incriminated "characteristics," the better to relegate them to their old place, while conveying to them that this place is desirable for women and men alike.[28]

What's dangerous about this development is not so much the theft from the women's movement as it is the disastrous, in part certainly conscious, misconception that the essence of the women's movement is something like "feminine experience," a holistic-intuitive apprehension of reality, back-to-nature. The militant content of the women's movement is concealed or removed if possible and the movement is misdirected and converted into an enriching way of life for men. The change is made palatable to us through the essential vehicle of a femininity that has been women's fate and against which large portions of the women's movement have fought in various ways – in the form of growing autonomy and independence from male global schemes for women, not simply in the form of an antithesis to the masculine.

Where in fact are women supposed to have gotten these wonderful abilities from, in the very bosom of the nature-destroying patriarchy, in these societies in which it's not only men who are severely damaged? How can this nature-oriented ecological life of women have come into existence? Solely from the act of giving birth? That's over soon enough, followed immediately by the great clash of

interests; mother and child run smack into the life-constrict-
ing and life-deforming traffic of social realities. Where is
woman's wholesome essence, steeped in her natural connectedness with life, to be found?

For my part I see in women more incomprehensible
criticism and shock – often vague and inarticulate – more
unassimilated grief, unassimilated and unlived life, than unity
with each other, children, and nature. Nature is no escape.
We cannot take designs from ecosystems in order to figure
out where to locate ourselves and how to exist. We cannot
simply fall into nature's lap and nestle there, that is, return
to the lap we've long since left. Nature today won't spare us
one single decision; because nature in no way embodies peace,
justice, equality, and freedom, going back to it cannot help
us. Nor can we safeguard ourselves by believing in a "scientifically" prognosticated imperative of natural development
for the better. We cannot safeguard ourselves at all.

In the present patriarchy that we inhabit, we must demand
of ourselves sharp-sighted and sharp-witted observation of
what is and of what was. And in the process it must strike
us that the friendly, appeasing, approving, head-patting assurance, "Women, you can remain as you are," represents
the modern version of doing away with women – our gentle
elimination. If we remain as we were and are, if we persist
in our secretly self-enamored powerlessness, then our remaining bit of future seems to me to be settled – then we
are running to our destruction and to our assimilation with
the self-destroying male.

8

THE FEMINIZATION
OF SOCIETY:
FEMININITY
AS DETERGENT
AND DISINFECTANT

T he biochemist Erwin Chargaff has recommended that all the researchers in the world commit themselves in writing to making no more discoveries from now on. He sees a total halt to research, a starvation diet for an indefinite period, as the only effective brake on the utter destruction of our future. The intentional absurdity of this recommendation shows how little this scientific researcher in his eighties thinks of the morality of his colleagues and of the good intentions of the institutions which pay them and employ them.

In any case Chargaff seems not to expect improvement from the champions of progress. Decontaminating the residue of presumption, ignorance, and megalomania is not something he seriously considers at a time when life seems more menacing than death and all thoughts of possible escape routes have begun to seem like sentimental nonsense.[1]

In his astute and acerbic thoughts on the situation, however, the category of the "feminine" as bearer of hope does not make an appearance. In this respect Chargaff is old-fashioned. A miracle is the only cure he won't rule out.

Today, anyone who is au courant can name this miracle: it resides in the feminine, in the female principle, in the female style or the feminine woman.

In many European countries a "feminization of political culture" has been remarked.[2] It forms the basis of hope for a more humane politics. Without a feminization of society "all of humanity can count on literally no future at all."[3] As we learn from the analysis of extraterrestrials who, after the nuclear death of the globe, put forth their interesting hypotheses about the causes of the catastrophe on earth: only the female inhabitants of the earth might have been able to achieve a political about-face before collective self-liquidation, a change in the fateful path; unfortunately, however, the uninfected ones were too weak.[4]

A certain masculine tendency toward the glorification and mystification of the feminine is of course nothing new. What is new is the designation of certain so-called female qualities as history-altering in scale and as attractive possibilities for male acquisition.

In the first wartime phase of this century, during and after the First World War, women, as the historically peaceful sex, were called upon by individual men to resist war. The proletariat writer Ernst Friedrich, for instance, appealed despairingly to them to prevent their husbands from enlisting, whether out of enthusiasm or obedience. Women were to tear up the rails, throw themselves in front of trains.[5] A bit later, Romain Rolland appealed downright threateningly to women to prevent the Second World War or else bear the guilt of murder: "If women do not fight this wave of annihilation with their last ounce of energy, may the blood of their sons come down on their heads."[6]

Today the male appeals are directed less to women themselves than to feminine qualities, to a historical projection in which men would gladly again share. Now it's not a matter of telling women to throw themselves on the tracks to derail men's destructive actions, but rather a matter of having women, patriarchy's non-disabled veterans, give a new cast to the values of those who hope for the future. Women should not necessarily themselves make an offering of their non-disabled persons, for in no case should they act alone, without men. Rather they should donate to men their wholesome qualities, their immunity to delusion, and do so as inconspicuously as possible.

There is scarcely a discriminating author who does not, at least in an introduction, subordinate clause, or footnote, see the salvation of Western culture and of Western man – salvation from his fragmented, doomed behavior – in the feminine, in contrast to the masculine. Even if hope in the female isn't new, scarcely ever before has so much political power to determine and reorient the future, to offset worldwide misery and existential impoverishment, been awarded to the female.

Those qualities ascribed to femaleness, the fantasy images of women, display astonishing consistency over a hundred and fifty years. This is not without its comic side, if you can still find any of this comical. The "extraordinary" nature of the feminine, which is situated beyond the masculine order of progress, exploitation, and expansion in a disorderly realm devoid of developmental logic, is still celebrated for its "creatively liberating qualities": emotionality, sensuality, surrender, imagination, sensibility, receptivity, empathy, harmony, patience, gentleness, understanding, and above all the capacity to love, to sacrifice, and to be selfless.[7]

When bourgeois sex stereotyping divided the spheres of the sexes, the ideological glorification of the female began to bloom extravagantly. With the development of the capitalist means of production, to be sure, the male saw himself as on the side of progress – of action, the public realm, expansion, importance, effect, the power of definition, of the production of a negotiable reality. But at the same time he saw himself as separate from the activities of women which, though unspectacular, seemed immediately connected to life processes. This female domestic praxis, which did not realize any commodity value or visibly follow any logic of progress, and so remained both unadulterated and unenhanced by fame and public actions, had been lost to men; it had vanished from their sphere of influence and inspiration.

Female activity was interpreted as the suppression of an essence that acts in accord with nature in constantly harmonious and repetitive sequences of events removed from any historical significance. Her work, which both played up and played down this essential nature, was seen as an activity without history or community. She remained mute, insignificant, and at the same time indispensable, and in her impulses, in her motive force, completely inscrutable to the male.[8] Her domestic activities seemed to the male to be integral and self-contained; they seemed to embrace the woman's whole person, weaving together body and spirit, feeling and reason, spontaneity and planning, communication and craft, beyond the great developmental logic of man's work in society, apart from the motive of progress comprehensible to him alone. What the woman did allowed men to progress without progress of her own.

The high estimation of "the feminine" recurring today surely feeds on the old hope that the historically female way of life contains something that patriarchal structure has forced out of the normal thoughts and actions of civilized male societies: an unspoiled treasure to be discovered, whose power has yet to be adequately exploited and determined; something which might go to waste, something man has not yet exhausted or penetrated, a treasure he does not find in himself.

The new incantation "feminization of society" conceals a collection of the seductive and the misleading. It covers a hodgepodge of male fantasy projections which all say more about men's intentions than about women's capacities.

It has a *soothing* effect in that it tries to prove with supposedly scientific argumentation that the reconciliation of the sexes has already been achieved, that women's protest is nothing but a relic from the past based on sheer fantasy.

It has an *unbalancing* effect in that it tries to suggest that women should back away from goals like autonomy and independence. These are distorted into "isolationism" and personal luxury and thus made into terms of political and moral reproach.

It has an *ingratiating* effect in that women are told, with obsequious expressions of gratitude, how influential and inspiring they and the women's movement have been for the current great change in thinking.

It has an *upgrading* effect in that women are awarded the competence and responsibility for bettering the world.

It has a *constraining* effect in that women are allowed to spread their goods around, to dish them out, but they themselves are supposed to remain as they are.

It has an *exonerating* effect in that men can continue their male existence while adding a few feminine accessories.

It has a *stupefying* effect in that the property in question here, the feminine, seems in its curative value to be intended for everyone. This foggy opinion emerges in the guise of analysis or knowledge, equipped with the most conciliatory directives: woman possesses a treasure, she should share it, and the man should accept it.

A contemporary example – representative of many others – is Roger Garaudy, French philosopher, former member of the central committee of the French Communist Party and 1981 candidate of the French "alternatives." Now that the working class hasn't gotten what it was promised, Garaudy sees in the feminine woman the revolutionary subject who is capable of rescuing a humanity which has slid into insurmountable misery. This hope and prophecy, of course, is tied to certain conditions: Garaudy urges the women's movement to move on from the demand for equal rights to the demand for the right to differences. Only in this way might women's riches come into use and man's dangerous atrophy and impoverishment – the consequence of his rationalistic detachment from the "fullness of being" – be turned around. Garaudy does not neglect to emphasize that these riches must in the end become a gift to man, to humanity, so that the future won't be a bane.

Woman's desired and necessary difference makes her a specialist of that end of the emotional spectrum which is free of all refusing, resisting, and negating impulses – the place where pure love resides. Even in Garaudy this love degenerates into kitsch. It corresponds to desires which betray what men would gladly receive from women and what they don't want to produce themselves. Woman, who "breathes in the rhythm of the world" and can establish a "vital relationship to the soil, to the living flesh of the earth," is to become again the loving creature, the great affirmer who defines herself "only in relation to others," who fulfills herself through unconditional participation in the life and sufferings of others and by "renouncing self-determination." Women thus are the only ones who might live up to an example in Western culture which men did not accept and could not follow – an example which for this reason could not in two thousand years overpower the patriarchal tradition: Jesus, with all his feminine qualities. Garaudy has wondered his whole life long that Jesus was not a woman. If he had been, it would have been more understandable why men didn't feel compelled to imitate him. The belated sex change of the divine man makes it easy magnanimously to bequeath to women an example which combines the great ideals of human love, consideration, and selflessness; ideals which it did not behoove men to realize but whose saving and healing effect they nonetheless do not wish to do without and which ought to remain in the world, animated and embodied by women.

With this transfer of the Christian ideal to women, men exonerate themselves of everything in their devastating history that they have committed and omitted. They call for the "liberation of woman" and for their own liberation through woman, imputing to women the noblest qualities, which are to make up for the atrophy of Western man. Men bemoan their own social and personal deficiencies – which they don't seem to notice until the moment when women prove to be not entirely congruent with the ideas of love delegated to them, when their contribution might rather consist in negating existing conditions; when man's possession of woman is endangered and his access to her is not assured; when he is not feeling well inside the shell of his manhood; when the reflection of male actions does not sufficiently appease him, when it may even frighten him. Then the female becomes the model of hope.

Another version of the feminization of consciousness is ingratiation. Wilfried Gottschalch undertakes something of the sort in his attempt at placating women and moderating sexual disparity.[9] His work is so stupidly impertinent that it would remain unbought and unread if it weren't exemplarily suited to those modish servilities toward women's liberationists and filthy gropings after a kind of femininity which are agreeable to so many men. Gottschalch's contribution to the reconciliation of the sexes operates through the psychoanalytic categories of envy and hatred. Psychoanalytic conceptions of sexual envy and their contribution to the theory of hatred are given a new argumentative direction in being clearly addressed to women. The ideological content is unmistakable. The argument explicitly pursues the goal of psychologizing into existence equality between the sexes and signaling to woman that her protest against male society and its representatives is nothing but sheer anachronism.

This pacification is supposed to succeed by way of a political change in the neoanalytic theory of "sexual symmetry." As early as the 1930s and 1940s (with Karen Horney, Ernest Jones) this theory criticized Freud's phallocentric perspective and introduced the mother's "omnipotence" for children of both sexes, as well as the boy's envy of the woman's attributes and capacity – thereby countering the one-sidedness of the supposedly universal interest in possessing male genitalia. As soon as this argument is transported from the anatomical to the social plane, thus theorizing the real asymmetry out of existence, it obscures substantially more than Freud's at least clearly androcentric vision. The latter mirrors – with involuntary clarity – the actual power differential between the sexes; Freud's ignorance at least reflects the actual asymmetry of the places occupied by the sexes and expressed in their self-assessment. Given this real asymmetry in the valuation and libidinous investment of the sexes' different anatomical properties, the penis can in fact be understood as a symbol for the position everyone, boy and girl, man and woman, would like to have – namely, the male position of power in a male society.[10]

The later attempt to equalize the initial psychodynamic conditions of the sexes and to turn them into their mirror images results in assigning the same psychodynamic roots to the gender hatred of both sexes, or even claiming that women have much less grounds for hatred of men than men have for hatred of women. For the infant's experience of the mother's omnipotence and the father's existential unimportance leads the boy to the bitter knowledge that he will never be able to be like her. The girl is spared this envious hatred, for she can gradually incorporate the mother's power into her own life; she only has to wait a little. Accordingly, masculine hatred of women is ultimately based on very special high esteem for the woman; the man's hatred provides proof of how admirable and desirable the woman is to him and how painful is the narcissistic insult of being excluded from her abilities.

Gottschalch's new edition of neoanalytic gender symmetry consists in the invitation for women finally to distribute envy and hatred among the sexes justly so that at least each of them has to carry an equal portion of this ugly load. After all, both of us, women and men, have the same problems with the fact that our bodies manifest the characteristics of only one sex. Women suffer from penis envy, men from birth envy. The penis symbolizes man's power, the ability to give birth woman's power. Only when one seeks the independence of the sexes from one another, as women currently believe they have to do, does envy develop for what she or he doesn't have. And because envy leads to hatred, women's hatred of men is the unnecessary consequence. So it should be recognized and acknowledged that men are dependent on women as are women on men; if you understand this you will be able to dispense with hatred of the other sex, all hatred will become transparent as an irrational wish to possess what you cannot have alone – but *can* have jointly.[11]

Men's embrace of such false emotional logic as natural, their clinging to an absurd mechanism of the origins of envy and hatred, shows nothing but their vital interest in ignoring the historically and substantively changing valuation of the alleged object of envy. It shows further the unbroken self-overestimation of the male, who apparently still can only think that what he possesses, his bodily, material, and intellectual property, is envied by women. It shows the unbroken logic of occupation – that naturally what others possess one also wants to possess and occupy oneself. Such misrepresentations upheld by men are striking; given the great dungheap men have erected, it would take some powerful emotional contortions for women to develop the urge to possess that as well and to envy men for it. This phony logic, that lack of possession leads to envy, envy leads to hatred – newly established as equally applicable to men and women – is now handed to women as a gift. They can be proud of the fact that their value has risen so much that enviable things can now be glimpsed in them. Such efforts at integration, such offers of equalization, serve to distract from the real reasons which ought to call forth women's real hatred and which surely can be explained least of all by envy of male possessions. If this logic of envy and hatred applies to the male, he ought to use his strength to uncover and then bury it. Instead, he manipulates arguments to try and commit women to the same mechanisms – as if it were a case of general lovable human failings, whose recognition might bring women closer to men and liberate them from the anachronism of gender hostility. The interests behind such efforts at symmetry are only too obvious: a nonexistent structural sameness of psyches is declared so as to pacify both sexes equally. In view of the power relations and historical experience which continue to exist, such efforts are politically and scientifically as foolish as they are dangerous.

A no less unattractive version of "feminization" is to be found in the recent bestseller by the music journalist and now "world scientist" Joachim-Ernst Berendt, a version which seems especially to arouse the enthusiasm of its large female audience. A central chapter of the work is entitled "Hearing Is Female." The author explains zealously and with arresting pathos that all languages in the world go back to an original language, to six original words, of which four are female. The primeval syllables of all languages, "the most powerful and creative," as well as primeval music, are female. The god of creation is female; what is heard and audible, taken in through our ear, what slips and slides into us, is female; all beginning is in the female uterus. "Female" conveys: cavity, orifice, hollow; it is the source of all things, all languages, all music.[12]

Here feminization means reducing woman again to the primeval orifice, defining her and paying her reverence as that original hole, instead of having to struggle with her modern desires for emancipation. This conception of woman seems today to have become a rare and desirable male role, for this primeval orifice is no longer what it was – no longer matriarchally powerful, no longer magically mysterious, but a body part with certain known physiological functions. And to obligate women to these functions again, and at the same time to celebrate her as the ultimate origin of all things, solves not a single one of the problems and disgraces women at present have to bear. It would, however, solve many of men's problems. First of all they could elevate woman again and keep her at a distance, respect woman as the Great Other and at the same time not be bothered by her. Second, the threat of women standing up for themselves and claiming their own would be eased if not averted. For a primeval orifice wants only to be used, to receive and to give birth.

In order to navigate through the tangle of prejudices, I will be concerned in the following not with the feminine as male wish fulfillment – which, measured by reality, is a phantom

– but with the aspects of this femininity that are realized by women themselves.

These unite in their attempt to live up to the male desires for femaleness. Woman's typically feminine qualities originate in her effort to imitate an image, the attempt to approximate her behavior to a phantom's and to echo male fantasy. At issue here is the appearance which woman herself presents to the world, which she herself carries out and lives; at issue is the often lifelong and life-absorbing attempt to behave like the model image. This "normal" form of femininity is an expression of woman's historical situation in the sexual relationship system and thus also the expression of a female morality which makes woman's existence into an existence *for* others, an existence geared to male handicaps. This order demands of women that they not harm men, and thus adopt a life of acting *as-if.*

In this acting as-if, existence for others becomes deformation for others. Women are supposed to act as if they are glad to be of service and available to others, to men; as if they take pleasure in men and in their dealings with them; as if they approve of and admire men's carryings-on; as if they are fulfilled and gladdened by the tasks and limits assigned to them; as if they know no contradiction, no negation, no hatred of their spatially and spiritually stunted life and those who cause it. Their existence for others has conditions attached to it, first and foremost the condition of protecting and supporting the men's world. Under this condition women are "rewarded for lying."[13]

Acting as-if requires that women maintain continuous control of their visible behavior, for no one must notice that this is a diversionary tactic, an outline in which the person is not entirely present. Women achieve their indispensability

to men and ensure their own protection by not expressing
– at least not directly – what they really think about men's
behavior, or at best doing so carefully, between the lines, and
with tactful packaging. In this way they simultaneously block
access to their own view.

Women's deliberate lies have succeeded throughout history
because, for one thing, it was in man's own interest not to
make much of an effort to find them out. On the contrary,
he gladly took them as the truth, took the facade as a gift.
He stylized it into women's natural inscrutability, even made
a general philosophy of "the ontological duality of myself
and myself in the eyes of the Other" in which the existence
of the lie confirms that consciousness is naturally hidden
from others.[14]

The refusal to investigate women's "as-if" thus results
neither from male discretion nor from stupidity. It is in the
man's interest, for his protection; for what he would discover
by exposing it would scarcely be flattering to him. Perhaps
every oppressor suspects this and curbs his curiosity.

Thus the opposite party, the man, gains the impression
that what's presented to him is in agreement with the woman's total person, with the inner structure of her consciousness; that what appears is identical with what the woman
really thinks. The echo that the liar's appearance, her semblance, receives, rewards the appearance. The liar passes off
the acting as-if as the reality of her person and profits
superficially – just like the man – from the habit of the false
echo, from the effect of the appearance, but not from the
person who arranges the appearance.

Such lying further succeeds because the staged "as-if"

is daily exposed to life, to training, to confirmation, while the person who remains behind with her intimations of how things really are, is not; she blurs shapelessly into the background. Lies that result from habitually orienting your own thinking and feeling to the measure of expectations and others' ideas of pleasure lead to self-incarceration. Your own knowledge is not simply a secret, hidden but existing alongside the as-if scenario; your own vision is not simply extended behind the scenes – instead, it never really comes into play. It remains diffuse, formless because unformulated. It receives no expression. It does not become present. It does not come into the world, and not really into your own world either.

So living a lie makes it impossible for the liar, with all her possibilities and potential abilities, to live. She does not expand. She forces herself and those whom she spares by deceitful reserve to stop short of approaching her real self; she prevents it from coming to light, even in all its inconsistency. She shows herself to be a conformist, displays only the part that fits in. Her presence is assimilated, cut back, like a facade. Women's relationship to this lie exemplifies an attitude with which women perpetuate their cultural and personal nonavailability, their self-marginalization. They become victims of their own lies.

Women in our culture have thus destroyed, perhaps have had to destroy, their intellect and feelings, by acting as-if. Their own experience and vision have been excluded from the world, or have never been called into the world to begin with, or have been falsified at the root. Women are in this sense "people without a world," people who have had reason to doubt their world, to doubt the reality value of their timid and invisible vision, and who have repeatedly withdrawn and assimilated it.[15] Every woman can sense that her world is not really hers, even if there are places reserved for her every-where. Women help to produce and preserve this world, but they are not really at home in it. They are included and admitted only under certain conditions. They live for a world in which others are supposed to feel at home. Many never-theless surely consider this world to be theirs, can imagine no other, want by all means not to lose it, just as it is. Many justify it through their endless efforts to belong.

The lie, the as-if behavior, is the way to belong and to disappear at the same time. It is a neat and effective means of not even allowing your own worldview, your counter-view, to arise, or of leaving it fuzzy and intangible, not to be grasped either by yourself or by others. "I am saying what you want to hear." The lie conceals, bends, denies, dilutes, distorts, takes back, sets aside, buries, glosses over thoughts and feelings, acts of thought and feeling, that really existed – or could at any moment really come to be. The liars cut from under themselves the ground where they could be their own persons, develop their own vision and present it to the world in full view. The liars remove themselves from the world. They prepare for their own disappearance; they work at their own disappearance.

At the same time this lie always guarantees that, with its help, you will be received into the world of female and male normalcy and gain admittance to those places where women are gladly seen. It offers certain rights of domicile in the men's world. The price is that you present yourself according to what is assumed to be reasonable for others, you anticipate the correction of your own experience and insight by the standard of what's expected.

The price is a conviction that your own person, as it really is, is not presentable. What's presentable is only the version which suits the others. I have to twist and camouflage myself so that the others will accept me. If I don't, I will win nobody's sympathy, I'll be rejected, I'll lose love, they'll find me out. To show myself as I am would be dangerous. I'd prefer to show an image of myself that will put me in a more favorable light with the others. What's present will be the forgery. In the end the as-if no longer conceals dissent behind the assimilated surface, but rather emptiness and the fear that perhaps there is no longer anything at all behind it.

Beyond the acting as-if, all of women's behavior, all "qualities" – whether or not they belong to the bouquet of the male-produced image of femininity – have arisen out of the existential injury to all women. Women bear the marks of their thousand-year-old circumscription and exclusion, as well as marks of their specific circumscription and exclusion since the beginning of bourgeois society. No quality can be separated from the conditions under which it was acquired and under which it is inculcated, lived out, and put to use. And these conditions are always the same: slavery and dependency, powerlessness and resignation, imprisonment and pain, revolt and exile, segregation and alienation, complicity and negotiation. No aspect of behavior can be thought of at all independent of these conditions.

When these qualities are isolated from their history to make them a "value in itself," as happens constantly today, it shows that the feminine continues to be regarded – even by progressive, leftist, enlightened authors – as an ahistorical construct. The projection of nature which women already suffered from 150 years ago is still going strong, though today it's been given new luster. For the equation of woman with nature today seems free of all discrimination – this at the very moment when nature is showing signs of revenge against her exploitation, when high technology is proving to be a giant flop and no longer fit for bolstering and uplifting male pride. Thus nature can no longer be seen as a boundless exploitable resource, but rather, compelled by the shock of her destruction, as property to be protected. The misunderstanding then spreads uncontradicted that saying woman is close to nature is the highest compliment that can be paid to her, or that she can pay to herself.

In discussions and critiques of the value of that cluster of qualities called "feminine" the question always arises of which qualities we should keep and which we should throw out. Aren't understanding, sensitivity, lovingness, and so on good qualities, ones that ought to be saved? Posed this way these are idle questions. The forceful exclusion of the requirements under which "female" qualities have arisen and have been and are being embodied in actual lives falsifies our view of them, allows us to forget that they are not transportable. Only in the abstract are all these qualities simply pretty. Empathy, for example, sensitivity, attentiveness, the ability to love and sacrifice, are not constants independent of relationships. At what social station are they present? Whom do they serve, whom do they use, who mobilizes them? For whom do they fail, fall through? For whom do they turn into their opposites?

First of all, the female qualities all follow the postulate of female morality which says not to harm others. "Others" are those for whom the woman is responsible in the bourgeois female domain, in the private realm, above all in the private realm of husband and children, at home. The instruction to women not to do harm thus primarily serves to protect the male from attack, from criticism, from questioning, from negation by the woman. It further serves to protect the woman herself, to the extent that she has reason to fear that overstepping or ignoring the male would bring her loss of sympathy, rejection, deportation, or life-threatening violence, and could take away her livelihood. The postulate exclusively serves the cohesion of the social fabric, especially of the family, for the woman's refraining from harm, from attack, from presenting her own view – to the point of losing it – secures at least an appearance of social harmony. By attuning her psychological antennae to what seems to be reasonable to men she prevents breaks in communication or at least postpones them, prevents separation from becoming visible. The moral training of women to do no harm thus serves first and foremost to protect male society from increasingly real criticism, and negation by women.

We have a tendency to regard this absence of harm as healing power – at least as a remnant of humaneness, as respect for the integrity of the other, male or female. This is not to be denied, as long as we turn this quality into an abstract one by releasing it from the concrete context of behavioral praxis, the social context of behavioral function. If we don't do this, then we cannot get around asking *whom* the woman spares and doesn't spare by her way of behaving, *whom* she harms and doesn't harm. These prized modes of behavior originate in a sequence of relationships, are component parts of a morality of relationships, which at its core always serves the male and the disparity between the sexes. All resulting behavior stems from this assignment of women to their restricted and predefined places in male society. All of it is born of an existential deficiency and of the intent to remove or conceal the personal and social deficiency, to avoid having to perceive it, or to convert it into its supposed opposite. Thus all the pretty qualities, like empathy, understanding, concern, patience, are not simply pretty. They are also a means of survival in the dependent position, a way to secure men's acceptance and affection, to earn and to keep their positive esteem, to compensate for their own existential devaluation, in short to obtain the right of domicile in male society. Woman's empty ego-spaces do not seem capable of being filled by their own contact with the world but rather – whether in fact or supposition – time after time, only by the bearers of social value, men, in their act of affixing value to woman.[16] These modes of behavior originated in the tragic game of the sexes. And the rule of this game on all levels is that the scale of values for the subordinate sex is fixed by the man. He is the determiner and definer of values. The resulting "feminine" willingness to exist in the world through him alone, to come alive through him alone, produces qualities which men may find pleasant, agreeable, and worthy of preservation. But we cannot evaluate their worth with a borrowed gaze.

"Masculinity" and "femininity" are historical sexual diseases. The addition of one disease to the other results not in recovery, but in spreading the disease, with continually new and surprising symptoms. The diseases can't be made more bearable, much less healed, by mutual complementarity. For the essential part of this disease is not the division, the halving, the non-wholeness, but the immorality of exploiting and letting oneself be exploited. The characteristics of the sexes are quite simply its result.

Men are trying to squirm out of this history. They want

to skip over their own criminal history, this long piece of work, by attempting to complete themselves with the "others," whom they themselves have shut out – that is, by finding in these "others" particles which seem pleasant, useful for whitewashing their dangerous defects. So they puff themselves up into an oversized creature, one male plus half a female, or one male plus one female minus slavery and minus pain – a new version of Frankenstein. The addition of "feminine" to male behavior, this questionable expansion of their repertoire, can at best lead to the short-lived appearance of a warm and fuzzy society with a hard core. In this society nothing would be right, though at first glance the man would be unrecognizable, as if his entire history had become a thing of the past.

9

CROSS-THINKING /
COUNTER-
QUESTIONING /
PROTEST

An editorial in *Feministische Beitrage* states that feminist research is about "a *different* way of acting, discovering, researching."[1] What can this mean, a "different" way?

A few men as well are demanding a "different" kind of scholarship, when for example they characterize the research of the last 150 to 200 years as the greatest colonial war in human history, as a punitive expedition against nature and people, who are steadily pelted by new barrels of knowledge trash. The sciences now prescribing a full stop, the researchers taking off the uniforms of professionalism and promising to halt all discoveries – for all of them, salvation from the sciences' giant scale, shameless expense, and rape of nature lies in a return to "small science."

This small, "different" science would try to unlock nature's riddles with the "key of love" instead of with the desire for money and progress or naked curiosity. It would not bag trophies or look for explanations; life would remain a wondrous mystery, and the researcher would never assume he could extract knowledge from this mystery: "Piety as opposed to pride, imagination as opposed to analysis." Such a science, instead of throwing a veil over reality, would "participate in a world which must be loved."[2]

To transfer such alternatives to a possible feminist research, to give in to such a seduction of the imagination, would be deadly. In fact feminist research is of necessity "small science," almost entirely without a financial base or public support, unable to challenge established positions or plunder nature, and this has nothing to do with modesty. Feminist research, which is fueled by the relations between the sexes, has little reason for a "loving consideration" of reality. It cannot escape or challenge the process of dehumanization by assimilation or through asceticism and a "positive spirit," but only by subverting, exposing, dredging up a badly constructed reality, and by revoking the piety and mystification that science is usually accorded.

The reality of the sexes is the bone of contention and thus the impetus of feminist research. So it is scarcely imaginable that the motivation for our questions can be tender care, loving penetration, participation in a beloved world: the description, observation, and appreciation of loved "objects."

"It would be heartening," writes Erwin Chargaff, "if all, say, twenty-year-olds announced their temporary withdrawal from humanity," if they decided "not to go along with the bloody circus."[3]

*   *   *

Women could not announce such a withdrawal, even if they wanted to. For women never fully joined; they were brought along. Men can always discard their works and those of other men, the miscarriages of the desire for knowledge. The malignant growth of what they produced can perhaps induce in a few men nausea at their own history, can in its excess bring about uneasiness and the "postmodern" wish for annihilation of the male ego. But women are not caught up in disgust at their own refuse, or in horror at their own transgressions. Because those are not their doing, women are now confronted not with the sovereign farewell task of discarding, but with the task of accusing.

The revolutionary achievements of male research justify concern for the future. Women do not own those creations. But they can't take any credit for this, for their lack of ownership is based on exclusion, not on choice. Men may have come to the point of demanding that humans should commit themselves in writing to making no more discoveries, but this does not apply to women. Women have yet to discover. . . . But what?

To research means to ask. What's "special," what's "different" about feminist research is the question itself: its origin, impetus, content, direction. What's important is *who* asks. For women what already exists is not normal; it is questionable from the ground up. What's "different" about feminist research thus lies primarily not in its specific methods or its "female-specific" content, but in the person doing the asking, and in her social status.

The questions throw things into question. They don't add to what already exists. They don't begin a process that ends with the solution to a problem, a methodology, an explanation, a next step, progress – trophies to be bagged. The questions are not impelled by certainty that an answer will be found, or by the search for success. They are also not, like their nobler counterpart, expressions of awe at mysterious beauty. They are outcries, or sometimes peals of laughter – from the point of view of normal science, unusual behavior.

Feminist research consists in women's continued investigation into this reality. It develops through questions – embittered, unabashed, agitated questions that arise from looking and listening. Its basic subject area is the world of male society – for there is no other – which imposes conditions on women's admission and station: reality, as seen from women's perspective. It includes the male constructs surrounding them as well as the male constructs imposed on them and female constructs imposed on themselves. Thus the material that fuels feminist research is shocking in nature.

The space which a woman takes up in this society, and the gaze she directs at what she finds there and at herself, reflect her attempts at admission and her orientation in a landscape where she is not at home but where she is nonetheless provided for. The effort to view the material of this life and its earlier history, to sort through it, to give it form, and to present it keeps running into external and internal hurdles. The view is not always pleasant, and so the gaze tends to welcome distraction. It is prompted by the same efforts at appeasement which otherwise support women's habit of making their life more acceptable. Subverting the images of femaleness and maleness has disturbing effects for all who do it. Thus even to think of possible subversion is already to be frightened, worried, and held back by its possible consequences.

Ten years ago, the concept of "involvement" came to stand for what was supposed to be different about feminist research. Involvement meant then more than subjective situation. It was an emotional condition or connection with a political position stemming from the fact that all women in male societies, regardless of background, race, and social class, have been made invisible, have been denied their rights, and bear the burden of a history that has reduced and distorted them. The common experience of sex discrimination was seen as having far-reaching consequences for women's research, which was to be supported by a common interest in countering powerlessness. Feminist research was thus the mouthpiece for all oppressed women, a way to give them a voice and to force fundamental changes in the scientific understanding of "man." This work could overthrow the power relations which the sciences installed between investigative subject and object. For in this light the investigator has neither the moral and theoretical right nor the personal and political motive for setting herself over the subject as one who knows, who knows more, who knows better. The "Postulates of Women's Studies" proposed by Maria Mies were supposed to designate that political locus from which the world becomes questionable to women and from which the experience of the norm of social injustice leads to an active scientific praxis: engaged, in solidarity rather than competition with colleagues, in contradiction to the scientific norm of value-neutrality.[4]

But the situation of the questioner is not thus adequately described, in fact it is arbitrarily distorted, simplified, and overstated. If women's studies has found it hard to follow its own postulates and if by now it can scarcely be seen to have existed at all, this is due not only to the inability of the individual researcher, or to the institutions standing in her way. In my opinion, it's also due to a false notion of social position, one that leads to a deluded, unrealistic self-perception.

Women, it is true, form an oppressed human group, but not one that has remained untouched by or immune to their circumstances. They are involved up to their ears in the very thing that weakens them, offends them, makes them sick. They are deeply infected. Neither their historical nor their present position is understandable if women insist on seeing it apart from men's placement of women at man's side and apart from women's assignment of themselves to man.

The locus of feminist research is not a clean and heartwarming place, not a noble, untainted position shared by those who come up short in society. It is rather a soiled and ice-cold place, steeped in and burdened by history, shame, and sorrow. It is not a place of affirmation and agreement, not even agreement among all women or unbroken agreement with oneself, but a place of negation and contradiction where women are not accepted, unwanted, rejected; for all that it's not easy to leave. Thus efforts at exposure and negation are directed not only to the misconceptions of the "outer world" of male society and its male representatives and perpetrators, but also to those misconceptions by women which make them co-promoters and co-perpetrators.

What this means for feminist research is that the impulse of solidarity, of "sisterly" commitment to women, as they are, does not become absorbed in social work for fellow victims of injury and oppression. Rather, it means radical questioning of our own sex and its secret understandings, subverting the construct of "femaleness" instead of upgrading it, elucidating those mechanisms by which women actively ensnare themselves in a net that forces or tempts them into invisibility and non-presence. It means confronting our own damaged and self-damaging history and present.

Thus feminist research does not restrict itself to "female-specific subjects." It does not just address what women do and think or did and thought, leaving the rest of the world untouched. Instead it asks fundamental questions about everything we take offense at, everything we want to get rid of, to subvert and expose, to drag into the light and make ridiculous, everything that we cannot believe and accept.

Feminist research cannot merely add to the answers of existing research, filling the gap and reducing the deficit by omitting and subsuming women. Feminist research does not fill any gaps; it is not a previously missing addendum to current subjects of research in the form of the un-cultivated or mis-cultivated female subject. It runs counter to these subjects. It is cross-thinking, counter-questioning, counter-seeing, contradiction, protest. It is thus also indifferent to the reproach of one-sidedness. As long as it doesn't reduce itself or allow itself to be reduced to what is "female-specific," it is not one-sided or half-true. It seeks to uncover the standardized systems, understandings, and lies of the andro-centric worldview.

This approach is "special" not just because of the con-sciousness and rage of woman as victim, who recognizes her exclusion from patriarchal culture and from the "subject" of history, but just as much because of the consciousness of woman as *accomplice,* who recognizes her inclusion and enclosure in this culture. Her contribution as the man's housemate and lover, as participant and coworker, as cofunctionary and affirmer of male deeds, as protector of male advantages, muse of male development, caring supporter, approving cothinker or silent partner, as both sufferer and upholder of male overvaluation and her own egolessness – all this makes her part of the subject of history, one that belongs and is excluded at the same time, a part whose questionable weight seems to disappear under the heavy weight of the male. This is evident not only in the male's ignorant, self-satisfied gaze, but also in the woman's tendency toward blurred vision of herself.

The female's complicity in the cynical development of civilized male societies consists – beyond any given historical change in appearance – in the "normal features" of the female social character, which guarantees the absolute affirmation of man and his world, in the specifically female acceptance of the perpetrators. This is conveyed by the woman's active and complex dealings as she buys herself a home base in male society by attempting to make herself unrecognizable as a negating subject. Woman's "complicity" means her active entanglement in the normal doings of male society.

Complicity is an analytic and moral-political category. To put it at the center of feminist questioning means, first of all, recognizing, setting out, and exposing patriarchal acts of force and men as past and present criminals. It means, second, analyzing woman's dealings with man and herself as actions oriented to the social criminal and his products, actions which may not be visible but are highly effective, indeed indispensable, contributions. Third, it means judging and negating woman's complicity, that is, taking a stand against it. When complicity is understood apart from the violent context of the crime and is no longer seen as women's systematic function for men's crimes, it turns into isolated female self-accusation and thus loses the character of protest. Women become perpetrators instead of collaborators; the view of power relations between the sexes as determined by patriarchal law is obscured. Insidiously, the woman makes herself the criminal. But complicity does not convey equal blame, and so it can't serve to exonerate men. (As if now finally, with feminist understanding, they had female criminals with equal rights beside them, instead of their own accusing victims at their feet.) Under the concept of complicity the man is the perpetrator of this devastating history, the woman the injured party. But her injuries do not simply diminish her and make her harmless. They are functionally contingent on what the man needs from the woman: her agreement, her loyalty toward his person and his crimes – her active need of him.

Understanding the woman as an active subject and revoking our consent to the violent relations of the sexes is the challenge for research that calls itself feminist. Otherwise women's studies will also become an "accomplice to the crime."

Up to now I have thought that the concept of women's complicity should not pose the question of guilt. I've changed my mind. The analysis of complicity does not, like the legal concept, assume consciousness of the crime, knowledge of the goal, dedication to its intentions, the will to commit the "criminal act." Instead of asking for empirical evidence of guilt, it asks about the character of the involvement of the woman as a patriarchally constructed sex within the overall historical complex.

The question of women's collective complicity is thus primarily posed independent of their individual knowledge and the consciousness that was historically possible for them. Looking back we can try to recognize with what effects, in what capacity, and with what behaviors women have done, not done, or helped to do something, without blaming them. Rightly or not, in looking at the past we shy away from naming the collective act as collective guilt, for the question of guilt presupposes the possibility of determining one's own behavior. We are not entitled to judge this if we don't know our own conditions of acting and refraining from acting, of knowledge and conscience.

But this does not apply to the present. We can see the result of the behavior of the sexes and can no longer spare ourselves the evaluation of its consequences. These are not remorse, repentance, punishment, or atonement, but the process of separating ourselves from the relations of agreement and affirmation, revoking them. Feminist abstinence and discretion about the question of collective and personal guilt, which arise from protectiveness toward the victim, incapacitate women as coparticipants in history and acquit them of making decisions compelled by knowledge of responsibility for their own actions.

The concept of women's complicity and shared guilt is not the destructive or self-destructive invention of a few present-day women fatalists.

In 1899, when women still had no access to German universities, a few tried to gain admittance to the university in Zurich, a gathering spot for German women students and feminists. In that year the Hamburg writer Ilse Frapan published "Monologue of a Bat," a moving account of enthusiasm and abandonment, disappointment, and a young woman's failure at a male university.[5]

"They tell us that woman thrives exclusively in the family. But,–has she prospered so splendidly? She hardens . . . mistakes the periphery for the center and despises what's essential. Her horizon is obscured with mere trifles (p. 40). . . . By forbidding us all free movement, they've made us small and then scornfully held up to us the narrow boundaries of the home as our whole world. And the guilt of the oppressor has become the shared guilt of the oppressed. By putting up with it, we've become flabby, sluggish, petty, short-sighted, superficial, and sly. We have even grown fond of our chains, we find ourselves graceful in our lack of self-sufficiency. . . . No, no, the way we are now, we are certainly not worth much (p. 50). . . . How many volumes could be filled with false accusations against women. . . . There was no church father so pious, no philosopher so wise, but that he had to tell a little dirty joke when he came to the subject of women. . . . And how did they respond to all the insults, all the suppressions? They persisted in loving the man and suffering for him and through him (p. 55).

This student of the last century is described as always driven, always restless, isolated, torn between hunger for knowledge, scholarly expectations, and despair at not being able to feel at home in the knowledge she discovers. At first she considers every moment of learning so precious and the knowledge that she's been deprived of till now as something "so wonderful" that the desire to assimilate, this "life of the mind," compensates for everything she has to renounce (p. 29). But after breathlessly hurrying through lectures and libraries, making a doomed attempt to catch up on what she doesn't know and to avoid literal starvation without the support of husband, family, or state, she departs from the place where she once felt reverence and anticipation. Yet not without a trace: her notes are to be read by those who come after her. These notes turn all their hopes to the women's movement as a movement of *enthusiastic* women: women who could get to the bottom of the growing mistrust of the value of existing scholarship: "we need new books . . . the old ones lie, they slander us! They're written by people who don't know us!" (p. 71). These women could at last take on "cultural work" themselves (p. 51); they, the unmarried ones, would have head and heart free for others, their idea of happiness would not be satisfied with two or three loved ones (p. 48); with their surplus of passionate feelings they would establish knowledge that would help them and other women; they would "strengthen and gladden each other" (p. 56); they would turn all their love "with glowing devotion and boundless spirit" toward the downtrodden (p. 48); they would be "advocates for their sisters" (p. 58).

To read this today is to feel ashamed. True, the conditions under which these visions of the future were devised are not comparable with those of the present. This almost hundred-year-old document is intended here solely to trigger the question of how the conviction of complicity and shared guilt is to be reconciled with the enthusiastic effort to reveal and revoke it, and whether the male domain of the university can be a place of such revealing today.

The university is a classic male institution, where the conventions of the male view of the world go largely unchallenged, regardless of how many women have penetrated it. This applies in principle to the human and social sciences as well, to scientific ways of viewing people and societies.[6] And yet these male-legitimated systems of thought are showing rifts and abrasions everywhere. The social sciences today do not affect economics in any way worth mentioning, and their political weight too has become slight. They no longer have a significant public voice and little power to shape opinion. Theoretically and practically they've been paralyzed ever since it became clear that social and political "crises" aren't visibly changed by societal analysis, social and individual learning processes, or pedagogical interventions. Work in these fields scarcely rests any longer on a comprehensive or even a less ambitious theoretical base. In any case, theories of emancipation which up until ten years ago still seemed to provide intellectual security, and to promise scientific and practical political insights, have been largely demythologized in a historical process that can hardly be reversed. The revolutionary content of the concept of mass, for example, has become questionable since the efficiency of technical apparatuses has eclipsed the efficiency of human mass and can lend monstrous power to the single individual and his solitary whims – called political decisions.[7] This theoretical dilemma puts many social scientists on the defensive. Many have lost their intellectual self-confidence. Some react with an aggressive defense and expansion of their territories, shamelessly raiding the treasuries administered by those who have affinities with them; some try to curry favor with the few outsiders, male and female, who with seemingly unusual ideas dedicate themselves to petty thefts; some retreat into industrious inconspicuousness, obeying the precepts of their guild; some also – let this not go unsaid – show themselves to be modest, helpful, and respectful toward those who are not like them, and do not turn their formal power against them. Most of them, however, remain sublime slaves. Scarcely anyone draws a conclusion. They ask no further questions, as if they didn't know what was left to ask. Nothing more occurs to them. Above all, they do not ask what is perhaps the only question left, namely, that of man's criminality in male society. An analysis of patriarchy, if it can't be avoided, is women's affair. This men find logical. Beyond this they fall back on their justifying norms and get stuck there, insulted or jealous, looking nostalgically back at their leftist past.

The prevailing social scientific norm is in any case not a unified whole and can't be encompassed by a single concept. The scholarly institution is also not simply a barricaded fortress with knowledge police asking for identification at the entrance, where deviants can pass only if they've got false papers or are wearing camouflage. The formerly monolithic power apparatus of science, a somewhat clumsy expression of cultural overdevelopment, is nonetheless also capable of mobility, also porous and brittle, prone to confusion and upset, deceptive, dependent on commerce and fashion, and diffuse. It can be killed off or revived. It consists on the one hand of men and some women who circulate and broaden the conventionalized views. But these views have to find listeners and buyers in order to spread; the purveyors can lose their customers of thought and knowledge. For these people are in principle able to agree with what's offered or to contradict it, to echo or refuse to echo; they can be bored or excited, come or stay away. What's offered needs takers in the university as well. And even if it's made into a compulsory diet, it won't nourish for long; it will reduce both donors and receivers to destitution.

Every definition of the university as a rigid fortress of male knowledge fails to acknowledge that wherever they go, women are in male society in all their fragility. There is no inside and outside; there are no gender-neutral domains or woman-free spaces either inside or outside the institution of knowledge. You can't be in a male world or a male enterprise inside the school walls and not in one outside them. Such a state doesn't exist. The scholarly institution is not fundamentally different from all other cultural manifestations of this society. And wherever women are, they determine by their own self-definition, and by their relation to what is professed, what they are and how they are to be seen, how and as what they are to become present. The developing curiosity about negation, the desire for knowledge about the historical right to knowledge and about counterknowledge, the intense and concentrated effort of thought, can lead to an occupation of this space which lends to the women involved not exactly sympathy, but authority. And the latter we need more than the former.

The enthusiasm of that student from our grandmothers' or great-grandmothers' generation was kindled by the idea that anything might be possible in the future – the idea of the unfettered woman. This woman would choose her own vocation, have the time to develop her intellect, and be free from the draining focus on the male. The expectations of the "amazons of intellect and enthusiasm" (Frapan) were synonymous with the beginning of their separation from complicity and shared blame, from consent to the stunting of the intellect and soul and the voluntary reduction to life as a human pet for a man.

Today it is recognized that being educated, earning our own bread, and remaining single haven't necessarily meant that women have expanded into life and put away their willingness to be depleted by men. Although women's struggles have since achieved much for us that was only desire and demand for her, the enthusiasm of that time has a stronger and more vehement sound than the rhetoric of today.

Today the source of enthusiasm cannot be the utopia of woman unfettered from man and his privileges, but rather the daily challenge of realizing it. This seems to be more difficult, more depressing, more wrenching than we imagined. Attempts at putting it into practice are met with blows and counterblows and run up against limits that are not only external but also personal. Besides, the present state of society is not exactly calculated to arouse enthusiasm for such attempts.

Yet one thing we no longer have need of today is the deference with which women at that time still approached the male place of knowledge. We see the "ailing monster" at whose sickbed we're supposed to gather, after "windows and doors were hurriedly closed to the world, to this wasteland that the monster has left us" (Claudia von Werlhof). Not only is it ailing and greasy, it is also apparently becoming more of a public danger the sicker it gets. For this reason, even if we break its spell and renounce our bowing before its secretions, we cannot completely overlook them.

Do women know too much today? Are we far too enlightened to still want (to know) something with enthusiasm? Is there no longer any knowledge we can be on friendly terms with? Have women given up on this research when they might have influenced it – making use of it for themselves, deriving from it subsistence for their own intellectual and spiritual self-preservation, treating it as a kind of cultural work on their own sex? Have the impatience of discovery, the euphoria of knowledge, disappeared with horror at what knowledge and discovery might and might not bring about? Are we growing tired from the strain or lack of strain associated with having no examples to admire and revere; does this diminish our ability to learn?

It is of course not surprising if we continually are crippled by loss of desire. This is not specific to intellectual work. It's a general fatigue, a "logical" response of the psyche as well as the intellect to the imponderable wastelands that surround us. But if we consider that this lurking loss of desire follows the same laws of necessity as other losses which we are asked to accept, then it becomes clear that it is the result of male society's mistreatment of this world and hence also a male mistreatment of us. It is a systematically perpetrated defect which, like other defects, is inflicted on us. And it becomes an aspect of our complicity to the extent that we do not try to oppose it. The theft of our passion for discovery would be one of the greatest triumphs of male society over its women: to take from us the passion for our cause. And to accomplish this not by the open use of force – for curiosity and enthusiasm are only in the rarest cases directly forbidden to us – but by getting us to do it ourselves.

10

THE PROHIBITION
OF HATRED

Thoughts without the prospect of a home, without a place to land, are sinister to women. We tend to allow ourselves to get involved in a thought only if its logic guarantees it a new resting place. If it does not, if it leads into imponderables, it is quickly pushed away, or not admitted in the first place. Such is the case with the question of our hatred.

Hatred is a solitary feeling, not a communal project. Thus the invitation to hatred affects many like an attempted seduction into insanity. Insanity, though, is both a step outside one's normal locale and at the same time a step inside – into the home, the hospital, to the nurse, the sickbed, into care that has the comfort of the familiar. But unlike insanity, hatred is not an escape from society and yet neither does it offer a new home.

An occasion for raising the question of our hatred is the Chernobyl incident. Just as we can scarcely imagine the dimensions of nuclear armaments, so we can scarcely experience the consequences of the radioactive meltdown. They are expressed in physical measurements, but our senses are

disempowered. It's not our senses that signal danger, destruction, or the proximity of an opponent. The basis for panic –
or equanimity – is a public information system operating
against the background of a physical and political system of
measurement. Knowledge, half-knowledge, false knowledge,
or no knowledge becomes the essential prerequisite for what
we feel and do. We cannot rely on ourselves, our information
is controlled by experts, people we don't think highly of, if
we think of them at all. Even if we were to put on a Geiger
counter and take it to the supermarket and into the garden,
it would be of little use, it would remain a toy, or a prosthesis,
something that only documents the failure of our sensory
organs to register what needs to be perceived. The alienation
is consummate. The word "independence" seems to have
become meaningless, synonymous with deception, ignorance,
or fatalism, nothing but a stupid fantasy or a blind desire. If
we turned off all devices, TV and radio, stopped reading the
paper, and instead turned to the "real world," took a look
for ourselves, what our eyes saw was: a splendid, immaculate
spring, blossoming pink hawthorn bushes and chestnut trees,
the first bees, mosquitoes, and flies, and people dressed in
summer clothes, hurrying on bicycle or on foot, by subway
or car, toward the beaming sun.

The non-sensory form assumed by the contamination
of those conditions essential for life shifts it to a realm that
is highly unreliable and menacing in its durability. Such an
event is not anchored in experience. It receives no confirmation from direct perception. In one of the countless TV
discussions when a moderator asked whether people were
afraid and how afraid they were, a man answered, "After the
news I've gotten I have no fears," and a woman, "I believe
the people who have learned their professions." Fear led

others to shower, clean house, hole up, or get away – not because they were more fearful, but because they gave credence to other information.

We can hardly test every piece of information. Our receiving apparatus can only sort and evaluate according to our trust or mistrust of the politics in play, of our sources of information. A sensor for the nature and the magnitude of the dangers of these times we do not have.

I kept feeling like a hypochondriac when the half-knowledge I gleaned about the presence of contamination turned the beauty outside into a deceptive facade, when the sight of spring and of children became torture, and the intake of information felt physically like an attack on what bit of *joie de vivre* remained. To insist on the invisible damage was somehow embarrassing, as if one were driven by a perverse lust for pain, sickness, and death. Only two weeks after the actual disaster doubts began to spread about the appropriateness of my own state of mind, as if I were myself psychically contaminated, a contributor to the contamination. Three days of not reading the paper and already I'm buying milk again; on the next day a new article on the effects of radioactivity on the body's biochemistry and a letter to the editor from employees of the Max Planck Institute for molecular genetics, and I'm taking the milk carton furiously out of my son's hand. On that same evening statements are issued by the Berlin Congress for Health and Science, all with the tone that anyone who is still worrying about possible dangers is at the very least hysterical. And already I begin to see myself as hysterical.

I'm somewhat more certain when it comes to anticipating the psychological consequences. When, for example, my thirteen-year-old son comes home from school with the news that a teacher said they could all count on not reaching thirty; when products from confined animals and closed-up rooms have become more trustworthy than what's been under an open sky: these are actual childhood impressions. This *becomes* psychological reality, whatever the biological consequences for the future of an individual body: life surrendered; nature full of lurking taboo and renunciation, storing up dangers from which humans should protect themselves; one's own room, where you try to collect everything you'll need for the duration; the utter abstractness of the causes of this sick relationship to the world.

The contradiction of the visible health of animate nature and the invisibility of its and our sickness, the uncertainty over the probability of this sickness, the interval of time before it becomes visible provide suitable grounds for that mechanism which enables and accelerates the development of the atomic age: repression. Our psyches, which tend to reinterpret visible reality if it's unpleasant, are certainly not ready to confront an invisible future reality if it's unbearable, least of all when the first excitement has passed and the event is no longer the number one topic of the day – no longer a conversational reality.

Reality operates in hiding and concealment. It becomes real only in a future where we cannot with certainty establish the causal connections to specific inventions and decisions, specific accidents and tests, specific amounts of poison in specific bodies of water, least of all the specific perpetrators. The long-term nature of the consequences renders them abstract to present consciousness. And with this, all talk of experience leading to knowledge becomes idle chatter.

But this very notion was one of the most important concepts of the women's movement. For it was women's experience that seemed to contain the critical material for opposing patriarchy. Experience alone seemed to dispute man and his law. Experience meant mostly bad experience. Now it becomes clear that experience also means *not enough* – that is, naivete, an impoverished and dilettantish capacity for knowledge. Having become increasingly devoid of contour and contrast, experience does not include the implementation of knowledge. Less and less does it supply what we need to know to say no to what's happening. So hatred becomes just as invisible as the thing it was supposed to hate.

Merely uttering the word "hatred" – one's own, that is – evokes frightened, reserved, or hastily deflecting responses. Women flinch. An unacceptable word. But I find no other word which better conveys the attitude of saying no. It's like the courage to do what's forbidden, which I need in order to insist on the word, even for myself. "But hatred is exactly what has made all this possible!" "The fascists hated." "Murderers, rapists, abusers hate." So go the objections, attempting to stifle instantly every thought of our own lack of hate, of the loss of our hatred. As if I'd allowed myself an extremely risky slip, a cardinal sin against the dependency of women on intimacy with what surrounds them. As if I were, myself, what I hate. Or as if there now arose the utterly personal, therapeutically easy question: whom do you really hate? What is the *real* object of your hate? What might your old childhood wounds of hatred have been?

Anger is allowed, outrage is allowed, and above all suffering, thus also hatred presented as childhood suffering, which casts its indelible shadow time and time again over the present; every emotion on the spectrum of love is desirable and above suspicion. Here you can lie to your heart's content. But hatred: here it gets serious. And if I go ahead and insist on the word, with no substitutes, then very soon there are no more objections. Silence prevails, and everyone hopes I won't come back to this subject again. We cannot think about hatred without immediately justifying it.

Hatred seems today to be – not as always, but once again – one of the most stubbornly taboo words. It may surface under the protection of therapeutic stresses and their psychic-theoretical underpinnings. A hatred which can be traced back to unresolved, unexpressed childhood feelings, to unavenged early wounds, is understandable; it is allowed, even encouraged, it must be "let out" and "worked through" in order to resolve itself into a variation of love. Hatred is always somewhat unmastered, it has nothing to do with its present "object," the monstrous thing that triggers it. The original figures, the eternal fathers and mothers, those who failed at loving or loved violently, they deserve it, it must go back to them, either directly or symbolically. And Volker E. Pilgrim, so he hopes and asserts, doesn't need to "hate" anything or anyone anymore, if he truly concentrates on himself and his needs.[1]

This result of psychoanalytic hygiene will please and relieve many, and will warm some hearts. Hatred is only the memory of hatred: it wants revenge on the original figures, on both of them. And all further or even new hatred in life is only a repetition addressed to the wrong parties. So in the present lives of adults, outside of ghosts from the nursery there is nothing to hate.

The tabooization of the word "hatred" as a *political word* has intensified in the last ten years.

Whereas in the 1920s "hatred of a society which treated people like dirt, like trash and rubbish," was a concept of resistance against a humiliating life and its causes, the materialization of National Socialist "hatred" made the use of this concept, beyond its psychological reduction, all but impossible for a generation.[2] As it crept warily into discussions during the leftist protests at the end of the 1960s, it could be used only after efforts had been made to delimit it and safeguard it from abuse and misunderstandings. In 1972, Dorothee Sölle attempted to make the distinction between "blind" and "productive hatred." She cited the statement of a social-work student from the documentary film "We Want to Make Flowers and Fairy Tales," produced by a group of Berlin students who had worked in an urban youth center at the end of the 1960s: "You know why I fight? . . . Because I hate you and you and you and everyone. I could beat everyone to the ground, everyone."

In this blind hatred, the enemy remains diffuse, the cause of the powerlessness unknown: "no authority figure . . . no one is there for him to relate to." He avenges himself aimlessly on every living creature for his own miserable, futureless life. Sölle sees this hatred as the result of the powerlessness of those who are victims of the contradictions of capitalist society and who lack elementary things like a place to live and to play, or fresh air – those who are only supposed to work, consume, and sleep, nothing more. To this blind hatred without hope Sölle counterposes "productive hatred," which she imbues with Christian social and political tradition. This hatred is "necessary for a new world."[3] Jesus was a hater who opposed human injustice with an unequivocal no. Hatred in this case is a human capacity which results in being able to commit, to recognize, and to distinguish between justice and injustice – and thus it plays a crucial role. Productive hatred, which is indispensable to making these distinctions, assumes identification with the victim and implies the struggle against injustice. The inability to hate is thus synonymous with the inability to comprehend suffering and to defend against injustice. According to this view, hatred grows from disappointment that is not forgotten, and from longing for another life that is not easily surrendered. The way to dehumanization is not hatred, but de-emotionalization. Productive hatred implies the ability to hold onto the idea of life for which it stands. Just like love, it evinces a longing for transcendence, for surpassing what exists. Sölle makes a plea for retaining the word "hatred," and not appeasing the provocation which this use of language contains.

Such thoughts were interrupted in the 1970s. One reason was the history of the Red Army Faction, its growing militance. It became *the* negative example of the left, a menacing reflection of one of the possible developments of the formerly communal revolt against the leaden times. It showed clearly where those who insisted totally on the total negation of existing circumstances were heading. Hatred was instantly equated with the act of annihilation: consistent hatred desires the annihilation of its object. Hatred fulfills itself in annihilation, annihilation results from hatred, annihilation allows the consummation of the annihilators' hatred. And when those who don't have political power on their side hate, then it is both murder and suicide at the same time. The RAF, which may have helped many "scratch out a dangerous path" and "better yet look for another way out" (Antje Vollmer) – better to ride the crest of the movement than be flushed down into the pit – became the great horror story of hatred as a force of destruction and self-destruction, and of the state's violence in reaction to it. When every attempt at understanding was seen as sympathizing with terror, and such sympathy became a life-threatening accusation, a complete ban of thought and feeling was imposed on the word hatred. Hatred and its depiction had to disappear, and they did disappear, without any reflection on the hasty, fearful equation of RAF with hatred, hatred with political deviation, hatred with personal disaster. In this coupling all unexplained and unasked questions were consigned to the generous territory of repression.

A further reason for banishing hatred as an "undesirable feeling" was the tendency toward a return to "humanity" in the ecology and peace movements and in parts of the women's movement since the end of the 1970s. The grandiose potential for destruction as a result of technological production and the critique of the ideological principles of those societies involved in it was accompanied by a call for feelings which eluded the mastery of so-called rationality. The longed-for rediscovery of buried feelings, it was hoped, would reveal the peaceful human essence, its life-sustaining interests, its love for others and for nature. Influenced by Mahatma Gandhi's ideas about nonviolent life and political action and the Christian teachings of peace, a broad discussion began about "positive feelings": they should be given more power, to correct and to heal. Women seemed specifically cut out for them. The valorization of femininity set in from many sides.

Some men and many women considered women, because of their biology, their social situation, their history or their psychosocial development, especially qualified for a loving and peaceful way of life.

In any case there is no hatred to be felt on the part of peace-lovers today. And if hatred, in some form or other, will not be denied – and the reality of human nature won't evaporate through sheer love – then it will be hurriedly psychologized, defined as a neurotic phenomenon in need of therapy. It will be brought to consciousness, treated, and worked through as a repressed relic of uncivilized or un-civilizable fundamental human nature. As a rule, it will be understood as a form of destructiveness, in league with aggression, anger, frustration, resentment, ordinary discontent and mental illness: a force which brings negativity into the world and should thus, to the greatest extent possible, be eliminated.

A completely different view starts from the assumption that hatred does not correspond to the present social condition. Hatred has become a historically obsolete feeling; with the development of long-distance weaponry and military technology of twentieth-century proportions, it has become expendable. The annihilation machinery of civilized peoples now functions on its own: waging and preparing for modern war requires no haters, only reliable bureaucrats, qualified technicians, and industrious workers. According to this way of thinking, the historical transformation or the historical reduction of hatred is supported by technologically determined changes in the male phenomenon of war. It is assumed that war is the special historical arena for hatred, in which the feeling is collectively organized in concentrated actions; hatred has no legitimate application outside of war and wars are the essential formative events in history, as well as in the history of feelings. With the disappearance of the old arenas of hatred, of hand-to-hand combat, of contact with the enemy following World War One, men also lost the feeling of hatred in battle. Feelings were superfluous, if not a hindrance; they might have vexed the mass annihilations of this century. The greatest and most perfect murderers of our century "were without hatred as they filled out lists, as they opened gas valves" (Sölle). Today hatred is an emotional luxury for which there is no longer any need, since the opponents have become invisible and the victims innumerable, their cries, their suffering, their dying unseen by the perpetrators. The temporal and spatial distance between action and effect, between murder and the technical use of a machine for annihilation, the incomprehensible number of victims make all accompanying feeling excessive. Hiroshima showed us both perpetrators and victims without hate: perpetrators without feelings toward the anonymous, abstract victims; victims without feelings toward the anonymous, abstract perpetrators.[4]

Günther Anders draws from these observations an untimely conclusion: the obligation to hate. Those "to whom it happens must, although they hate hating, nonetheless hate. . . . Whoever does not hate the infamous . . . brings upon himself the suspicion of being its bedfellow." The disappearance of hatred is more dangerous than the feeling itself was. "It's this very hatelessness, the inability to hate, it's this very deficiency, that's going to be the ruin of us."[5]

This conclusion is infectious. I'd very much like to take it up myself, though this would throw everything into question again. For how can women make this conclusion their own, when they and their history were not included in the analysis? What does the conclusion have to do with women? Can they be subsumed? Can we simply join in? Is the hatred we've been discussing a male phenomenon, and do we have to produce our own genealogy from our own history? It can't be that women lost their hatred – if in fact they did – for the same reasons as men. Then why did women lose it? Did they repress it, do they have memories of a long-lost hatred, or do they have none? What does it mean that women do not know the hatred of male hand-to-hand combat? Does the one disappear if the other proves at some time not to be necessary? What does it mean that women have not participated, at least not directly, in the male shaping of hatred? Could this be women's privilege? For what has been exhibited to us we do not want to imitate. The following reflections are merely a careful posing of questions which might enable us to think further.

The realm of normal femininity features very little hatred or negation. For these require that the person oppose her environment actively and singly, that she separate herself from her opponent in the consciousness of being an individual.

But the visible behavior of women reveals more readily their powerless or successful work at trying to create harmony, with the aim of belonging, of warding off exile. The tendency to assimilate to the existing constellation of power, the tendency to disown their own will for the sake of alien ideas, the deep insecurities when disorientation threatens, the continuous impulsive giving to men, whether cautious or spirited; the addiction to mirroring others and the always attentive fear of loss of love and affection, often engraved in their faces, voices, and postures – these betray the effort to reconcile conflicts and to gloss over contradictions. That isolating confrontation with the environment presumed by every expression of hatred seems to be avoided with every possible kind of behavior. If a weak ego is the fundamental defect of constructed femininity, then woman would be less expected or feared to negate what exists and surrounds her; "subjects with weak egos [can] endure no separation from the community . . . hence no being-for-oneself in otherness."[6] Male society expects from woman the affirming and protective gaze at her surroundings. The negating woman would steal the ground of her so-called identity from under her own feet. For by saying no she would no longer be who she was, or she whom she was there for, no longer belong where she was.

Women seem to have had little training ground for negation in male society. But hatred, like all other feelings, is a sociohistorical phenomenon which comes to life through practice and training, and which, through social employment or disuse, either stays alive or mutates and disappears. Negation needs an arena, a field of application, so as not to become superfluous, expendable. But women's history exhibits few arenas for hatred and negation which are legal or legitimate for women. Marriage, the principal way of life for women in bourgeois society, their principal place of residence and the personal history of most women today, no matter how they now live, can never have been an arena of hatred, a praxis of negation, for women. No doubt marriage was and is a more or less secret battleground of the sexes. But despite violence, dependency, and infantilization, despite cunning and spite, it is not negation we find within the intimate sexual relationship. Woman cannot negate the persons and structures by which she also orients herself. She cannot make this battlefield the constitution of her ego as man has been wont to do; at war with his opponents, he constantly discovered new proving grounds, large or small, and used them to integrate himself into society with a strong ego and growing self-confidence. There is no parallel to this in women's recent history. The person who is needed for the constitution of the ego cannot at the same time be negated or hated. Any time that women became serious about saying no, it caused a patriarchal breakdown; it was a deviation and a derailment, resulting in exile, destruction, or pathologizing – unless the woman took the separation into her own hands and exiled herself. Negation from women is a socially unnecessary attitude, an unwarranted feeling without any foreseeable application. Male society has no need for the hatred of its women.

What was desired and allowed in any event was reliance on male models of hatred, hatred under male governance and purview. Through men's glorious and legal opportunities for hatred – which were rewarded with the highest recognition by nations, communities, and many women – women could potentially participate in men's hatred and direct it toward the same enemies as the men. It could be that this deputy position was for women's benefit. It could be that they identified with the male haters to whom they otherwise looked up, that part of their feelings was somehow involved in the old body wars, that somehow they were able to side with them, to psychically act with them. But this participation of women, the yielding or annexing of their feelings to agents representing them and, on the part of the men, the grateful borrowing from and depletion of their emotions – this contract of abdication between the sexes expired at least forty years ago.[7] Now women were drawn directly into war, exclusively as annihilation material.

What was desired and allowed was hatred which women could direct at themselves and each other. Even if this can in part be written off as literary invention – no great imagination is required to guess why it pleased the male mind when women fought among themselves, preferably with the motive every man understood of fighting over a lover – still the fact remains that women have at their disposal a rich and proficient repertoire of ways to say no to women, that to use them is less risky than to say no to a man. But negations among women all follow the principle of depreciation, of equal devaluation in the protection and shadow of the fundamentally guaranteed approval of the man.[8] To this extent the "hatred" of women by women does not contain that moment of separation, the solitary ego-identity. Its motive and function are not comparable with those of male cockfights, male acts of annihilation, nor with what is being sought here.

In recent years women have done much themselves to substantiate and verify the diagnosis that women are void of hate. This happened not with the intention of exposing the defectiveness of this supposed or desired fact, but rather with the aim of obtaining for women the moral ticket of admission into the normal world. By defining women as qualified for peace and void of hate – which once again anticipates the equation of "peaceloving" and "without hatred" – women try to procure evidence that their own sex is capable on psychological and moral grounds of participating in those precincts of male society that have historically excluded them. This evidence provides the assurance that these precincts will certainly not be sullied or derided, or be shot full of holes. By their ability to influence men toward the good, women seek also to legitimate themselves. Thus they try to document empirically and to analyze psychogenically the fact that women have fewer impulses of destruction and violence in this life, that they bear hardly any seeds of evildoing within them – at most those learned from, borrowed from, transplanted from men, thus only in pathological instances. Women's psyches are completely integrated; nothing dangerous lurks in their depths. The psychogenetic background is almost clean of destructive impulses. So women can daringly and yet without danger be incited to aggression, aggression with a handicap, with conditions – with forethought and afterthought, and with allowances made.

The proof of women's "betterness" is attempted through evidence of their hatred-free psychology and their sociability, their moderate behavior and their social harmlessness. One method is to claim that women generally tend to repress feelings less than men.[9] This statement implies that the feelings which women bring to the surface do in fact constitute the feelings of women. They have no more. Men apparently still hold something back; there are still mist, secrets, dark primordial bogs to discover. The claim that women live out their feelings – that little is hidden, walled up, or falsified – imputes dull or limited feeling to them. But the history of women is precisely the history of repression: the repression of all inappropriate, undesired, explosive, exploding-out-of-male-space feelings, of feelings that negate what exists.

Men used to go on about female feeble-mindedness. Women today are unwittingly doing the same thing. The claim of a weaker repression mechanism and a weaker need for it on the part of women represents a modern parallel to the old diagnosis of feeble-mindedness. It takes the existing condition as a given and raises its value, not thinking that women are capable of saying no. Such a fatal claim seems to confirm the "eternally boring in woman" and Nietzsche's shameless question: "Has any woman ever herself confessed to the shallowness of a female brain?"[10] At least men have conceded that had women not been rendered harmless by circumstances, they would in reality be "highly dangerous."[11] Women seem not to suspect this of each other.

All this talk of peaceableness exposes the interest in producing an assurance of reliability in the indisputable behavior differences between men and women, in securing female-specific competence for at least the better and more constructive behaviors of the two. This intention is assured of a broad consensus. Women allow themselves to be betrayed with the help of a general seal of approval for their own sex. Once again they expect to find a niche for themselves through their gender. They want to make their own acceptance and value contingent on a ready-made, authorized, respectable, official rehabilitation. The peace-loving claim contains an indirect prohibition of hatred. It wants to take away women's evil eye. But this is one means of acquiring knowledge. The self-interest that sees evil, the passion of hatred that sees through false appearances, are veiled by understanding, sympathy, lovingkindness, and care. Without hatred for portions of this culture and its people, men and women, we are not sufficiently shaken up, not deeply stirred. Hatred is an indispensable maxim against this culture – not just the contemplation of goodness without a trace of aggression. Without passionate negation we become dispassionate toward the existing state of affairs and we fail to recognize hostility because it doesn't really interest us.

The peace-loving claim also spares women the pain which hatred always causes. It arouses fear of this pain, and prevents insight into the fact that hatred must be learned and fed by looking at and confronting evil. For this it needs no artificial nourishment, what's at hand is enough. The peace-loving claim attempts to withdraw this nourishment. It supports what history has demanded of women and habituated them to, namely, not to develop the desire to say no, and instead at best to share in an alien emotion as they follow male comrades in hatred.

Hatred was forbidden to women because male society could not use it and exploit it and because it could have become uncomfortable and dangerous. Hatred was allowed to women as long as it remained bound to male privileges, as long as it adopted the judgments of the male. Women themselves fear their hatred because its negation of closeness frightens them too deeply. Women themselves prohibit it because its absence seems to promise that they might be admitted to places where till now they have rarely ventured. Hatred is made more difficult for women because sensory experience – their familiar domain – does not supply the "whole truth." The women's movement itself makes it more difficult, as long as it advocates a flattened-out concept of experience which pretends that perception is unmediated.

Such a concept of experience does not contain the expansiveness which once belonged to it: the activity of experiencing, exploring, researching, informing, and investigating, in order to become "experienced." What can be experienced by women in this society, experienced passively, is a restricted space in which the atrocities of reality are admitted only as singular, individual, piecemeal, fragmented, random, and discontinuous, and mingled with nice feelings too. But the concealed reality of the present is not recognizable as a whole in this notion of experience and its flattened content. This content, with all its contradictions, does not suffice; it can't be jolted by real experience. It contains too little challenge to arrive at any judgments from out of the welter of perceptions and sensory impressions.

Hatred, as it is meant here, is a category of *judgment*. It is not blind rage; rather it brings lucidity. Hatred requires reason as much as passionate feeling for the sake of continuity and reliability. It is an unconditional passion in the face of what should not be; it is the wish for the nullification, for the nonbeing, for the ought-not-to-be of what ought not to be, because it can be recognized as bad. It is a moral challenge to that patriarchal hygiene which acts to prevent the negation of those portions of the world which need negation by women – for without women those parts will never be negated by anyone. This negation does not make "malignant creatures" of us, it does not make the person as a whole "negative." For the motive of negation is always the passionate comprehension of harm: I want something not to exist and something else to exist; I want something not to exist so that something else can exist and not be harmed.

This feeling, which can be called love – passionate arousal through the visualization of harm – is not spectacular and does not seek strength and security; it sees the inconspicuous and finds value in what has never been noticed before.

11

THE "MORAL
INSANITY"
OF WOMEN

An investigation into the murders of husbands by American women in the nineteenth century reached the following conclusion: most of the proceedings against women who poisoned their husbands ended in acquittal.[1] This unexpected verdict in favor of the women rested on the fact that the men sitting in judgment were unable to imagine any motive for a woman to kill her husband. The men – judges, prosecutors, defendants, jurors – started from the stubborn conviction that women by nature, if they are normal, love men. This assumption led them consistently to ignore those living conditions, those feelings, which caused women to stir arsenic or strychnine into the tea, the whisky bottle, or the chicken soup of the unsuspecting spouse. The acquittal was an expression of the men's interest in self-protection, and specifically of their own prejudices about themselves. The normalcy of these women, who did not look like witches or crazy people and who were able to point to lives that were as orderly as they were difficult, that is, average lives – their indistinguishability from all other inconspicuous and devoted wives made their conviction as murderers of men impossible. Criminal conviction would have meant official confirmation of their deed, and thus also public confirmation of the fact that every average woman carried in herself the possibility of finding her average husband, who had committed no worse crimes than other average husbands, unbearable. This compelling conclusion would have been so threatening for the husband, it would have entailed such an all-embracing self-critique and questioning of relations between the sexes, that every man who insisted on the unalterability of such relations – and thus on the unalterability of his person and his privileges – had to favor dropping the whole matter and dismissing it as unspectacularly as possible, by acquitting the woman.

Men found it more reassuring to blame a man for such a crime, while concealing the possible motives of the woman. It was surely better not to rack your brains over it. The woman's acquittal was the price male society paid for continuing to labor under the illusion that all women were on their side. There were 541 known cases of murder by poison in England alone in two years; this figure aroused fear in men, setting in motion both fear of female revenge and the compulsion to ignore it. The "protection of the law" was supposed to uphold a certain social ignorance. And so men are shocked by any mention of an especially repulsive offence against female blamelessness – not by the crime, but by its exposure.

One means of preventing exposure was the diagnosis of "moral insanity" or "moral dementia": an irresistible impulse which suddenly overpowers the woman's moral orientation. A temporary moral defect, a moral disengagement, suddenly muddles the woman's firm standards of good and bad, but she remains otherwise intact, for she seems to still love the man, the man she poisoned; she cries at his funeral, she behaves thoughtfully and in good housewifely fashion, she speaks no evil of her husband, the neighbors experience nothing untoward. In fact, everything is just fine. Except one day she went out and bought rat poison, waited for a time when he wasn't feeling well due to alcohol or indigestion, and took this opportunity to come to the rescue with her bottle; the family doctor had already indicated intestinal inflammation or indigestion and was then simply perplexed by the sudden disastrous worsening of his patient's condition or embarrassed by his own evident misdiagnosis.

The invented concept of moral insanity, which in the legal sense exonerated the woman – temporarily – candidly betrays a great deal. It betrays a society's complete lack of understanding regarding the real situation of the woman, who takes up arms against violence by seeking to get rid of the agent of violence. It also betrays men's horror at the possibility that women might draw conclusions from their fundamental fear of their husbands – namely, the conclusion that they *do not love their husbands.* That women can reject men must remain unthinkable. True, women suffer at the hands of men, this is their female profession; but that this suffering can lead to refusal, to saying no to men, this must remain unspoken, inconceivable, unimaginable.

The diagnosis of moral insanity thus reveals a whole ideological net which man throws over woman, namely, the structure of patriarchal female morality. According to this morality, woman is a creature who is moral "by nature," at least when she is healthy – indeed, a creature equipped with a higher morality than man, because she is able to love man under any circumstances, come what may. Men's violence thus becomes a challenge to the woman's capacity to love.

In spite of everything he does to her, normally she does not hate him, she does not hurt him, she does not come too close to him, she lets him be just as he is and wants him anyway. Woman's morality proves itself in her love for a man with all the attendant disappointments, blows, wounds. In fact, these are what make love truly valuable – they make it what it is. The "higher morality" of woman, attested to by men, has its basis in women's idolization of the opposite sex, or else, when that sex proves too obviously not to be very godlike, in their doing everything to make it more closely resemble that image. Man believed that woman was created to counteract men's mistakes and thus to make him into a more complete human being than he otherwise would be. A woman was never to reprimand her husband or to argue with him; instead she was to compensate for his deficiencies by way of her behavior and to influence him through sensible and tireless amiability. In keeping with this task, woman, ever since the rise of early capitalist society and the bourgeois family, has been a *moral model*: the moral mother of her children and the moral leader of her men. The criterion for the moral function of woman was, again, her capacity for affirmation. Female morality means saying yes to men. One thing was and is expected of all women of all levels and classes, that they not only look after their men with food and a cozy home, but morally support them and arm them, that is, convey to them day in and day out: that's good, you're good, keep doing that, you're irreproachable, you're fine, you're perfect.

A woman who knew how to live her moral code convincingly offered proof of the rightness of the male sexual ideology of bourgeois society, according to which women are *completely different beings* from men. With her morality of affirmation woman proved herself to possess virtues which simply aren't at men's disposal and which they therefore mustn't strive for – virtues which at the same time are not anything women have earned, for nature has given them to her. Helpfulness, self-control, self-denial, peacefulness are not results of woman's efforts of will and feeling, not a result of work on her own person, not an expression of submitting to the inevitable, not an expression of fear or of rational calculation that an argument might bring her into bodily danger and so she must do her utmost to avoid one; no, they are an expression of her beautiful feminine essence, about which she can't do a thing. Thus women are not humans who act morally, they simply *are* moral. They make no effort, they make no decisions, they make no sacrifices, they make no distinction between protective and destructive actions. Thus no special respect needs to be paid to woman for her strenuous good behavior, no special gratitude. Her lovable, harmless, pleasant behavior has nothing heroic about it and is not to her credit; she is simply gratifying an urge, fulfilling an instinct.

The causes of the rare failures of these male-affirming instincts have never been sought where they would be found, in the behavior of men, but rather have been sought in an acute and mostly reversible disease of the moral immune system, a disease in which the experience of male violence pathologically fails to lead to more love and love despite everything. Moral insanity was a certificate which temporarily saved women from the scaffold or life in prison, so that men could go on living under the illusion that under normal circumstances they were loved by women, no matter what they did to them. At the same time "moral insanity" was a euphemism for the phenomenon that women *can* give up their affirming, tolerating, forgiving, or even just ignoring attitude toward male violence; that women can abandon female morality along with the affirmation of men demanded of them by male society and decide to attack man's fundamental convictions. This non-affirmation is the most dangerous threat to his personal and social existence, a threat that touches so directly on the foundations of male self-confidence and self-definition that it was supposed to remain unspoken, veiled in magical silence, and not to arouse that otherwise wide-ranging male curiosity.

Is this simply an anecdote out of the nineteenth century? Can man continue to uphold the deception that he is under all circumstances loved by women? Do women continue to uphold the appearance that, apart from short but dramatic moral absences, they will stick to the rule of affirming the male?

A leap into the present, first into the metaphorical realm of film – specifically, Dutch director Marleen Gorris's "A Question of Silence." One morning, while shopping in a boutique, three women who have never met before murder a man who is a complete stranger to them, the boutique owner. They do it without planning, without arranging, without preparing, without dramatic cause, not in spontaneous self-defense, not out of emotion, not in a raging collective bloodthirsty attack, but rather coolly, calmly, silently, slowly, almost matter-of-factly, casually. Just as calmly they then leave the store, each in her own direction. The rest of the day each woman does something she has always wanted to do. In the detention center, they meet again.

The search which now begins for the motives for this

murder finds no verbalized answer. The three accused women have nothing to say about it. They are silent, or they talk about anything else, but as to their motives not one of them utters a single word. The psychiatric investigation, entrusted to a well-meaning, painstaking, competent woman, comes to the conclusion that these are "normal" women of various ages from various social classes. In the hearing the psychiatrist also refuses to evaluate the women as crazy or to certify them as temporarily insane at the time of the deed. She insists: these are completely normal women. This meets with general annoyance on the part of the court. To the evaluator's pointed remark that in coming to its verdict the court might take note of the fact that the perpetrators are women, the state attorney says yes, the fact has not escaped him, but it is legally irrelevant. The murder victim could just as well have been a woman and the three murderers just as well three men. This sentence triggers laughter – first from one of the accused, then from the second and the third, and finally irrepressible laughter from all the women in the courtroom. In the midst of this laughter, the murderers are led away, still laughing. They do not speak of their motives, but every woman understands them, and no man understands them. The helpless and aggressive search for legal grounds for the deed finds in this laughter its only answer – a speechless one.

What is threatening for men about this sinister conspiracy of women is their normalcy. They are not mentally disturbed, not manic, not rebellious, not feeble-minded, not down-and-out; they have children or husbands, they are intelligent or talkative or reserved. They lived the lives of average women *and* they murdered a man. To see this simultaneously is unbearable for a man, unthinkable – it cannot be. It means every wife, including his own, could one day reach for the clotheshanger or the hatstand. Every woman could one day hit upon the notion of getting rid of her husband, her boyfriend, her boss, or any strange man, or even just find him disposable and expendable or entertain the desire for his absence – and without grounds, for this murdered man had committed no crime; he had only discovered a woman shoplifting and discreetly confronted her. As for the other men in the film: one hadn't much to say to his wife, as little as she to him; another was dumber than his secretary, but thought a great deal of her competence; a third had answers to everything before answers were possible; others spent the nights with their wives in such a way that gave their wives no cause to repeat it. In other words, completely average men. What could the motive be?

This uncomprehending question is the really revealing question. Examples of understandable motives would be jealousy or disappointed love. These prove the strength of feeling for the man, that a woman is crazy for a man. Or greed, which proves that a woman can chase after the same things as men do. Or self-defense, which proves that women, like real men, are willing to put their lives on the line in a duel to protect body, honor, and property. But this murder lacks any motive.

In reality this story probably never happened. It is a blueprint for the conflict between the sexes which in the present time has come more and more clearly into consciousness: the difference and distance between woman's view of man and man's view of himself. This is a metaphor: women murder a man, men cannot understand why, and these women are not the least bit sick; they're in their right mind, in full possession of their faculties. They murder him as a *representative* of all men. It is a generalized rejection, not individual self-defense or revenge against a single evildoer. A representative act against what all men have in common: taking things away from women, owning everything, determining everything and being in charge of everything, and having no consciousness of what this means for women or of what women really think of them.

From the metaphorical present of the film, a leap into the real present: in the second half of this century, the normal violence of male society assumes a new form. Sexual violence, wife abuse, rape, are historically old "ways" men have with women, which keep cropping up in new guises. But violence is not only what the individual male does to the individual female who has come into his possession or who places herself at his disposal. Male violence has found a generalized form in which it becomes independent of the single male individual, whether violent or peaceable. In 1986, for example, it materialized primarily for European countries in the insensible, invisible form of the renewed release of radioactivity – the consequence of thinking that everything that can be done can also be justified.

The example of the plutonium industry makes it clear how, through great male technologies, this earth our home is in the process of being brutally destroyed. I want to highlight what is already well known. The reactor union, Germany's biggest producer of nuclear reactors, whose president announced that after Chernobyl we live in another world, was at the same time preparing to export four atomic reactors to Spain, Argentina, and Brazil, and is counting on further orders from Yugoslavia, Egypt and China. If, as can be expected, five hundred reactors will soon be operating on the earth, together with their estimated probable accidents, then we can count on a meltdown about every twenty years. This means the calculated acceptance within a single generation of three to four of the "largest probable accidents" along with their insidious consequences, whether death or exponentially multiplying disease. These five hundred nuclear reactors are designated in the *Handbook of Atomic Energy* as "trifles" compared to the more than fifty thousand atomic bombs which are at present stockpiled on earth.[2] Even in the event that these weapons are never deployed, the constant threat of so-called peaceful use remains. In the case of a failure of the cooling system in a reprocessing plant, the radiation released to the population in a radius of one hundred kilometers could be ten to two hundred times the fatal dosage, a destructive effect greater than both world wars put together. In addition to this, the radioactive waste produced in reactors and reprocessing plants and through nuclear tests and accidents will always remain somewhere on the earth, for a period of up to twenty-seven thousand years. This waste, like other lethal poisons, is somehow disposed of, which means they try to get it out of sight – washed into the rivers, blown into the winds, sunk onto the ocean floor, hidden in tunnels: out of sight and out of mind, stored away and repressed.[3] Still it can reach every cell, fill up any space; it is invisible and can creep in everywhere. Humans and other living creatures who know nothing of the dangers cannot recognize them. No separate warning system exists for them. The insensibility of the violence confounds our instinct for danger. Until a future time unimaginably distant from the generation which caused the damage, all descendants should be cautioned against having faith in the earth their home, where the products of violence are buried.

I am not concerned here with the question of what degree of real danger is linked with low-level radiation or to what extent the fears that have arisen might be based on panic and hysteria; nor with the question to what extent fear of the statistical probability of an increased cancer rate in central Europe, in light of a completely different kind of misery experienced by people of the Third World, might be an emotional luxury of prosperous societies. I am not concerned with self-pitying complaints about the once again restricted menu for the coming winter, nor with the packrat mentality which spread among many West German citizens, male and female, in the early summer of 1986. I do not, in other words, mean to discuss Chernobyl in terms of the intensification of individual precautions and calculations of survival.

What concerns me more is to confront – beyond all personal fears – the question of what the unimpeded development and spread of powerful and deadly technologies mean for the relations between the sexes, for woman's view of man as a social category, a socially constructed Western human type. This violence, which both exceeds and falls short of the limits of what an individual can experience, this annihilation of the earth as a potential "home" for its inhabitants, is *man-made*. The endangering and destruction of the future, of life and places for living, is the result not of innocent or merely negligent acts, but of the deliberate actions of male societies. It is not only geographical areas that have become threatened and inhospitable. Trust in the human beings who represent these societies and their habits of thought – and these are men – has been damaged, damaged pervasively, just as an individual woman who falls victim to daily violence and devaluation by an individual man will slowly abandon her trust in him.

This universal violence was designated by women after the Chernobyl incident as a hell which was created and invented: a hell which consists in the fact that man has engraved in nature a danger he made himself, so that it now appears *in fact* to be the enemy which it has been declared to be since the beginning of modern times; that disease becomes the norm, food unenjoyable, luxury trash, devotion surveillance, protection control, and beauty afflicted with concealed menace.

Claudia von Werlhof writes, "The horror at this glimpse into hell is concentrated gradually into pain at the sight of children. . . . Already they are after him (the three-year-old), greedily, icily, indifferently, insatiably. Already they want his life. . . . It reminds me of how in so-called kiddie porn the victims get younger all the time. . . . I know that they are already after him for themselves, in school, in the military. But I'm not yet prepared for this. I, the mother, have already been eliminated, pushed aside. . . . The child doesn't have a chance anyway. He'll just be plucked away. Even while he's laughing. . . . From now on we have to expect that this life, since it has been weakened, is delicate, perhaps sickly, and not long for this world. . . . That we will survive our children. . . . They've messed up the children, just like that, incidentally. . . . The child was just an unimportant matter, an ancillary risk, something that just happened to come up. . . . Human sacrifice in its most horrible form, namely the sacrifice of children, has been essentially reinvented, generalized. . . . What is happening with my child seems like something sexual to me, something masculinely sexual, sexually violent: I keep thinking, 'What pigs they are, what pigs they are!' I feel the way the mother of a violated, raped, tortured, threatened, and beaten child might feel."[4]

I cite this passage not because I believe such feelings and existential political accusations are reserved for mothers. It is not a question here of the condition of motherhood, or the uniqueness of the love between mother and child. It's more about the vehement emotion of love, which, it seems to me, seldom finds expression today. It is a question of being shattered by damage to life; only those who know love for other living creatures, whoever they may be, can be shattered by this. Perhaps love for the really innocent, the unsuspecting, for those who are simply harmed, is the strongest impulse of despair, rage, and clarity. And a clear view of reality arises not only from sympathy with the injured, but from identification and condemnation of the injurer.

The more unequivocally women perform this identification and condemnation, the greater will be the discrepancy with the feminine moral code of affirming man. The potential love objects are dwindling. In the social figure of man there is less and less to be loved.

The feat that's expected of women – namely, to say yes to male society and to love its exponents, men, in spite of everything – becomes an act of emotional acrobatics which can be performed only under the grossest misapprehension of reality; not without an extravagant exaggeration of feelings, not without phony perceptions and sensory illusions, not without reality-deforming mystification. Diagnosis: delusionary denial of reality, imaginary wish-fulfillment with subjective certainty.

This male society seems to be on its way to driving its women into collective "moral insanity," according to our initial definition – that is, to bringing about the feared negation of men themselves. And this is the only prospect held out by the violent developments of the present: that women will finally separate from the patriarchal female morality and its core – the fundamental, irrational, no longer justifiable, delusionary affirmation of men.

Such a separation leads inevitably to experiencing, consciously and on a daily basis, our *homelessness* in male society. If the non-affirmation of man is more than merely a private thought, more than a theoretical insight, if it leads to confrontation with almost every assumption about male and female, then the number of places where we can feel we belong contracts and our homelessness becomes apparent.

Home is a complex word for affirmation. It is always coupled with the past, a return to what has already been experienced, a glad remembering, the desire for and joy in repetition. But the reactivation of feelings connected to or associated with the past becomes painful or unbearable when there is no more going back to these places we once affirmed – because we have had to cut away the path, or because in the light of our present perspective these paths have lost their memory value. When every memory is connected with sorrow, when we look on stretches of our individual and social history with only melancholy or disgust, then any instinct to settle down in them is exploded. The German past already contains so much that is monstrous, for those who do not try simply to slip out of its personal and political interweavings, that it actually takes some insensitivity to feel at home in it. Moreover, in every slice of history women are confronted with so much that is suppressed, neglected, violent, submissive, with so much humiliation of their own sex, that embitterment and estrangement, not the desire to settle in, are their first reactions. Our history does not hold a selection of memory spaces for us which we can symbolically return to and where we are free to stay. We can experience this estrangement every evening at the end of the TV broadcast day, when our sisters intone the national anthem at the top of their lungs: "fraternally" for unity, justice, and freedom for the German "Fatherland." At least this estrangement remains relatively external. We can get over it personally; for presumably our identity does not unconditionally depend on being represented in the anthems of this nation. As always, this equanimity too betrays a great deal about the problem of where we belong.

Where is our home? What does home mean for women? Can we know our home?

On the one hand, women in male society are fundamentally homeless. The world in which they live is, as a whole, not their world. To be sure, women are indispensable companions. They enrich and enhance, complete and embellish male days and nights, male residences and sometimes also workplaces, male desires and fantasies. They have their tasks and functions, which no man can or will take from them. But they are not at home in this world. For it is a world for man, built and unbuilt by him for his own interests, for his ideas of life and love, for his products. Women have no place here which is their own.

On the other hand, women do not normally live as homeless vagabonds, as psychic hobos, deportees, or exiles. On the contrary: the home which they try to make for others is identical with the world which is granted to them. This is their territory. And the woman of bourgeois society was the center of this territory. Woman as home-maker thus has a place where she belongs and where she places herself: at man's side. Women have a right to a home in male society, albeit with conditions: women have and find their home with man to the extent that they say yes to him; they have and find a home in this society to the extent they say yes to its man-made-ness.

The contradiction here – to be at once socially homeless and historically situated at man's side – exposes the paradox that pervades the concept and the feeling of home. Women need the prescribed and sanctioned retreat because in general they have no other space to call their own; because in fact they do not belong outside, and the road is no trustworthy place for them to stay; because they know their way around best at home; because this is their workplace; because they have learned to regard it as their realm of responsibility and all other areas as less important and not in need of their efforts; because for these reasons the home is filled and beset with most of their memories, experiences, and feelings; because, in addition, it is difficult or dangerous for women, as the less muscular and generally unarmed members of this society, to live without protection; because they are the ones who are publicly offered as bait for male lechery; because they believe themselves to be defenseless.

But on the other hand, this abode, where perhaps once something like the origins of life were to be found, is also a place which is threatened and endangered, where violence penetrates into the subtlest regions of the psyche and the most intimate parts of the body: a secret scene of the crime or a ghetto. A place that throttles life and inspiration, a place of asthmatic narrowness, distress, and overcrowding, that prevents experience and reduces competence. A place stuffed full with fetishes which replace living connections. Here is where woman normally settles down, here she finds her nest.

Some essential features of home are missing here. Home and violence are mutually exclusive. The places at men's side are not islands in the midst of a dangerous surf or an anonymous desert. The nest is not made of different material than its larger environment. And even the elimination of violence does not result in home. Without free movement, without coming and going, appearing and disappearing, surprise and discovery, recognizing and being recognized – as a matter of course, not something that leads to a frightened closing of the inner and outer eye – woman's place is only an apparent home, and the relief of knowing her way around gives way to disgust at the all too familiar shell and the short-sightedness of the woman inhabiting it.

So for women the phenomenon of home is beset with much ambivalence. Sometimes we look in despair for a psychic place where we could settle down again, for memories which we might keep, for people we were with before. Then again we bristle at all our efforts to put down roots. Then there is no place and no feeling which the word home corresponds to; we are rootless, uprooted. After a brief contentment, instead of homesickness comes wanderlust, and it all begins over again. Do we really need something like "home"?

What about women who do not look to man for their mental or their emotional territory? Women who reject the paradox of wanting to find something in a place where it is not to be found – like the drunk in the joke who is looking for his lost key tirelessly and in vain under a streetlamp, and to his friend's question whether it wouldn't make more sense to look somewhere else says no, it's too dark over there.

Where does it lead, this parting with man the apparent home? There is no place to hide, not even a fleeting one. We can't have the home we really wanted to go back to. It is not a place we can visit again, and not one we were forced to flee to. We were not expelled from our homelands. It was *our decision* to leave.

But since not having a place at man's side has been, at least during the era of bourgeois society, a decision without culture or tradition, life as a homeless person is unfamiliar and unmastered. Life with the genuinely homeless, namely women, won't lead to a new home for a long time. The women's movement has, I think, proved rather than disputed this. The hope of living among women, with a network of our own, is not fulfilled automatically, simply, or quickly. In attempting to find a home, almost everything by way of a bad reputation that clung to the old home can creep in again through the backdoor. Or there are other unexpected surprises. The devaluation of woman is not only a crime of man's, it is also often a hidden offence of women. The discarded past forms of our personalities aren't cast off with impunity, and so in women's attempts at home-making often one main thing is missing: continuity, being able to return unconditionally, the staying power which accepts the passage of time kindly, generously, and calmly.

As homeless people by choice the diagnosis of "moral insanity" applies to us. But today we can't depend on male society to continue to supply the formerly exonerating aspect of this diagnosis, so as to protect itself from the truth with the fog of incomprehension. It is too late for this. Relationships have become clearer. Perhaps, too, our exoneration would not serve the cause of clarity. The "end of male society" begins with the increasing breakdown, with our *breaking down* the insane yes-saying to man which has accompanied the development of this civilization and has given it the dynamic of a lethal avalanche. This insane affirmation of man in all its covert and overt, secret and public forms is becoming unparalleled in its madness. And so we are forced to turn things around. Women suffer from collective moral insanity if they accept the meager right of domicile proffered to them along with recognition from those who cannot and will not help us, except on their terms. To see that we are alone and that every home is a gift, not a normal state of being; to see that homelessness is not synonymous with paralyzing catastrophe: this is perhaps the most honorable condition, the spilling-over of unbound feelings – spiritual and psychic vagabonding.

NOTES

Author's Preface

1.   See Susan Sontag, "Mind as Passion," in *Under the Sign of Saturn* (New York: Farrar, Straus and Giroux, 1980), 197.

2.   Peter Bichsel, "Ich bin meine Heimat," in Jochen Kelter, ed., *Ohnmacht der Gefühle: Heimat zwischen Wünsch und Wirklichkeit* (Weingarten, 1986), 178.

3.   Marlis Gerhardt, *Stimmen und Rhythmen: Weibliche Ästhetik und Avant-garde* (Darmstadt: Neuwied, 1986), 19.

4.   Klaus Trappmann, ed., *Landstrasse, Kunden, Vagabunden: Gregor Gogs Liga der Heimatlosen* (Berlin, 1980), 71.

5.   See Erwin Chargaff, *No Serious Questions: An ABC of Skeptical Reflections* (Boston: Birkhauser, 1986); Elisabeth Moosmann, ed., *Heimat: Sehnsucht nach Identität* (Berlin, 1980), esp. "Sehnsucht nach Identität: Schwierigkeiten, mit Heimat von links her umzugehen," 30–71.

6.   Gerhardt, *Stimmen und Rhythmen,* 108.

1. The End of Certainty

1.   Thomas Mann, "Death in Venice," *Death in Venice and Seven Other Stories,* trans. H. T. Lowe-Porter (New York: Knopf, 1936).

2.   Peter Sloterdijk, *Critique of Cynical Reason,* trans. Michael Eldred (Minneapolis: University of Minnesota Press, 1987), 131.

3. Friedrich Nietzsche, *The Birth of Tragedy and The Genealogy of Morals,* trans. Francis Golffing (Garden City, N.J.: Doubleday, 1956), 291.

4. Ernst Bloch, *The Principle of Hope,* vols. 1, 2, and 3 (Oxford: Basil Blackwell, 1986), 3.

5. Joachim Schumacher, *Die Angst vor dem Chaos: Über die falsche Apokalypse des Bürgertums* (Frankfurt, 1978).

6. Jean-Paul Sartre, *Being and Nothingness: An Essay in Phenomenology and Ontology,* trans. Hazel Barnes (New York: Simon & Schuster, 1969), 181.

7. I refer here specifically to music because it is always an event in time, always in the present and always ephemeral. Through its own laws it can convey a world liberated from the weight of daily stupidity. It has more physiological urgency than visual and verbal art products can claim. Music can call forth feelings and states of mind which we would never know without it.

8. See Stefan Andres, *Wir sind Utopia* (Dusseldorf, 1950).

2. In Abhorrence of Paradise

1. Herman Hesse, "Brief an einen jungen Deutschen" (1918), *Europäische Dokumente,* ed. R. Schneider-Schelde, vol. 5 (Munich, 1946), 9ff.

2. E. M. Cioran, *Geschichte und Utopie* (Stuttgart, 1979).

3. See Karola Bloch and Adalbert Reif, eds., *Denken heisst Überschreiten: In memoriam Ernst Bloch* (Frankfurt, 1982).

4. Ernst Bloch, *Träume vom aufrechten Gang* (Frankfurt, 1978).

5. Ernst Bloch, *The Principle of Hope,* vols. 1, 2, and 3 (Oxford: Basil Blackwell), 24, 25.

6. Bloch, *Träume vom aufrechten Gang.*

7. Hanna Levy-Hass, *Inside Belsen,* trans. Ronald Taylor (B&N Imports, 1982).

3. From Deception to Un-Deception

1. See Joachim Schumacher, *Die Angst vor dem Chaos: Über die falsche Apokalypse des Bürgertums* (Frankfurt, 1978); Sigmund Freud, "Thoughts for the Times on War and Death," *Civilization, War and Death,* trans. John Rickman (London: Hogarth Press, 1939).

2. Ingeborg Bachmann, quoted in H. Holler, ed., *Der dunkle Schatten, dem ich schon seit Anfang folge: Ingeborg Bachmann* (Munich, 1982), 83.

3. See Günther Anders, *Die Antiquiertheit des Menschen,* vol. I (Munich, 1980), and *Hiroshima ist überall* (Munich, 1982); Robert Jungk, *Die Zukünft hat schon begonnen* (Rienbek bei Hamburg, 1952), and *Strahlen aus der Asche* (Reinbek bei Hamburg, 1980); Horst-Eberhardt Richter, *Alle redeten von Frieden* (Reinbek bei Hamburg, 1981).

4. See Günther Anders, *Die Atomare Drohung* (Munich, 1981), 120.

5. See *Kursbuch 68:* "Furcht und Zittern" (Berlin, 1982); see also the special issue on war of *Ästhetik und Kommunikation akut,* vol. 8 (Berlin, 1982).

6. See official documents such as SIPRI, *Rüstungsjahrbuch 1981–82* (Reinbek bei Hamburg, 1981); Alfred Mechtersheimer, ed., *Nachrüsten? Dokumente zum NATO-Doppelbeschluss* (Reinbek bei Hamburg, 1981); Palme-Bericht, *Bericht der unabhängigen Kommission für Abrüstung und Sicherheit* (Berlin, 1982); The United Nations, *Kernwaffen* (Munich, 1982); Reinhard Kaiser, ed., *Global 2000* (Frankfurt, 1980); Migel Calder, *Atomares Schlachtfeld Europa* (Hamburg, 1980); Mary Kaldor, *The Baroque Arsenal* (New York: Hill & Wang, 1981).

7. See Christa Wolf, *Lesen und Schreiben* (Darmstadt: Neuwied, 1980), 233; Martha Mamozai, *Frauen in deutschen Kolonialismus* (Reinbek bei Hamburg, 1981).

8. Irene Stoehr and Deterl Aurand, "Opfer oder Tater? Frauen im I. Weltkrieg" (1), *Courage* (Nov. 1982): 43–50; "Opfer oder Täter? Frauen im I. Weltkrieg" (2), ibid (Dec. 1982): 44–51.

9. See Michael Kidron and Ronald Segal, *The New State of the World Atlas,* rev. ed. (New York: Simon & Schuster, 1987).

10. See Alexander Rossnagel, *Der Fall "K": Szenario über den Atomstaat im Jahre 2030* (Essen, n.d.).

11. See Hans-Günther Brauch, *Der Chemische Alptraum* (Berlin, 1982).

12. See Arnim Beckmann and Gerd Michelsen, eds., *Global Future: Es ist Zeit zu handeln* (Frieburg, 1981).

13. See Jack D. Forbes, *A World Ruled by Cannibals: The Wetiko Disease of Aggression, Violence, and Imperialism* (Davis, Calif.: D-Q University Press, 1979); E. M. Cioran, *Gevierteilt* (Paris, 1951; Frankfurt, 1982), 51.

14. Günther Anders, *Die atomare Drohung,* 55.

15. Maria Mies, "Weibliche Lebensgeschichte und Zeitgeschichte," in *Weibliche Biographien,* no. 7 (Munich, 1982), 54–60; see also Mary Daly, "Spirituelle Politik oder die Göttin ist ein Verb," *Courage* (Dec. 1982): 16–19.

16. See Annette Kuhn and Valentine Rothe, *Frauen im deutschen Faschismus,* vols. 1 and 2 (Dusseldorf, 1982).

17. Reprinted in Gudrun Ensslin and Bernward Vesper, eds., *Gegen den Tod* (Stuttgart, 1981).

18. Ingeborg Bachmann, "Simultan," in *Werke*, vol. 2 (Munich, 1982); Sigrid Schmid-Bortenschlager, "Frauen also Öpfer – gesellschaftliche Realität und literarisches Modell," in Höller, *Der dunkle Schatten*.

19. Ingeborg Bachmann, *Essays, Reden, vermischte Schriften*, vol. 4 of *Werke*, (Munich and Zurich, 1982), 275.

20. Compare Frigga Haug, "Erziehung zur Weiblichkeit," in *Frauen-Formen*, H. Höller, ed., *Argument*, Sonderband 45 (Berlin, 1980), 85–94; "Opfer oder Täter?" *Argument*, Studienhilfe SH 46 (Berlin, 1981).

21. Gabriele Wohmann, "Wörter mit Temperatur," in Ensslin and Vesper, *Gegen den Tod*, 104.

22. See Ti-Grace Atkinson, "In der Falle der eigenen Phantasien: Weiblicher Nationalismus – lesbischer Separatismus," *Courage* (Aug. 1982):26, 28; Gisela von Wysocki, *Weiblichkeit und Modernität: Über Virginia Woolf* (Frankfurt, 1982), 9.

23. Mary Daly, *Gyn/Ecology: The Metaethics of Radical Feminism* (Boston: Beacon Press, 1978).

24. See Silvia Bovenschen, *Die imaginierte Weiblichkeit* (Frankfurt, 1980), 158ff.

25. See Marlis Gerhardt, *Kein bürgerlicher Stern, nichts, nichts, konnte mich je beschwichtigen* (Darmstadt: Neuwied, 1982), 128ff.

26. Jutta Heinrich, "Der Luxus nicht hinzusehen," *Courage* (May 1982): 33; *Mit meinem Mörder Zeit bin ich allein* (Munich, 1981).

27. Christa Wolf, in *Berliner Begegnung zur Friedensforschung: Protokolle des Schriftstellertreffens am 13, 14 Dez. 1981* (Darmstadt: Neuwied, 1982), 116, 117.

4. Love and Lies

1. Barbara Rohr, " 'Kinder helfen siegen': Aus Feldpostbriefen meines Vaters an seine Töchter," *Dialektik: Beiträge zu Philosophie und Wissenschaft* 7 (1983): 2, 3. Quotations are from the manuscript.

2. Frauenhaus Köln, *Nachrichten aus dem Ghetto Liebe* (Frankfurt, 1980), 105.

3. Herman Göring, cited in Georg L. Mosse, *Der nationalsozialistische Alltag* (Königstein, 1928), 114.

4. *Hirts Deutsches Lesebuch für Mädchen* (Breslau, 1939).

5. I wish to thank Susanne Stern for suggesting that I look into this question.

6. Martin Gilbert, *The Final Journey: The Fate of the Jews in Nazi Germany* (Mayflower Books).

7. Paula Silber, *Die Frauenfrage und ihre Lösung durch den nationalsozialismus* (Wolfenbüttel and Berlin, 1933), 22.

8. Magdalene Rohr (née Ehmann), *Mein Leben,* (December 1986), 52, 92, 93.

5. The Last Outbreak of Love

This essay was written for the collection *Lieben Sie Deutschland? Gefühle zur Lage der Nation,* ed. Marielouise Janssen-Jurreit (Munich, 1985).

1. Ingeborg Bachmann, "Wir gehen, die Herzen im Staub," *Werke,* vol. 1 (Munich, 1978), 11.

6. Feminism and Morality

1.   Jutta Brauckmann, *Die vergessene Wirklichkeit – Männer und Frauen im weiblichen Leben* (Münster, 1984).

2.   Friedrich Neitzsche, *The Gay Science,* trans. Walter Kaufmann (New York: Random House, 1974), 181–82.

7. The Turning Point

1.   See Rüdiger Lutz, ed., *Bewusstseins (R)evolution: Öko-Log-Buch 2* (Weinheim, 1983), esp. Dieter Duhm, "Gewaltlosigkeit? Versuch einer Antwort," 182–85; Marilyn Ferguson, "Wir brauchen ein Weltgewissen" (interview with Peggy Taylor), 72–79; Fritjof Capra, "Krise und Wandel in Wissenschaft und Gesellschaft," 27–35. See also Rüdiger Lutz, *Die sanfte Wende: Aufbruch ins ökologische Zeitalter* (Munich, 1984); Dieter Duhm, *Aufbruch zur neuen Kultur* (Munich, 1982), Marilyn Ferguson, *The Aquarian Conspiracy: Personal and Social Transformation in the 1980's* (New York: St. Martin's, 1987); Fritjof Capra, foreword to Marilyn Ferguson *Die sanfte Verschwörung: Persönliche und gesellschaftliche Transformation im Zeitalter des Wassermans* (Basel, 1983), *The Tao of Physics* (New York: Bantam, 1984), and *The Turning Point: Science, Society, and the Rising Culture* (New York: Bantam, 1988); Joachim-Ernst Berendt, *Nada Brahma: The World Is Sound* (New York: Destiny Books, 1987); Hazel Henderson, "Thinking Globally, Acting Locally: The Politics and Ethics of the Solar Age," *Woman of Power* 11 (Fall 1988): 13–17.

2.   Lutz, 1983, 11.

3.   Ibid., 75.

4.   Ferguson, 1987, 29.

5.   Lutz, 1983, 173ff.

6.   See Capra, 1988.

7.   See Duhm, 1983, 182–85.

8.   Duhm, 1982, 66.

9.   Peter Passett and Emilio Modena, eds., *Krieg und Frieden aus psychoanalytischer Sicht* (Frankfurt, 1983).

10.   Henderson, 14, 16.

11.   Capra, 1983, 14; Capra, 1988, introduction and conclusion. See also Henderson, 192ff. In a recently published foreword (Lutz, 1984, 7–10), Capra dispenses for the first time with the rhetorical formula on the meaning of the women's movement, which would not have found any resonance in the book he is introducing.

12.   See Capra, 1988, 226; Lutz, 1984, 105; Ferguson, 1983, 226.

13.   The concept of entropy, from *tropos* (Greek: transformation), comes originally from thermodynamics and refers to the tendency of physical systems to approach a state of disorder; "the degree to which relations between the components of any aggregate are mixed up, unsorted, undifferentiated, unpredictable and random," Gregory Bateson, *Mind and Nature: A Necessary Unity* (New York: E. P. Dutton, 1979), 228. Also used in the figurative sense of unbounded change, disorder, chaos.

14.   See Lutz, 1984, 10ff.

15.   Capra, 1988, 45.

16.   Ferguson, 1987, 228, 227, 226.

17.   Henderson, 189.

18.   Lutz, 1983, 159.

19.   Michael N. Nagler, "Friede als Paradigmenwechsel," in Lutz, 1983, 157.

20. Ibid., 156.

21. Ferguson, 1987, 32.

22. Capra, 1988, 303.

23. Lutz, 1984, 103.

24. Capra, 1988, 339.

25. Capra revises this – again only rhetorically – in his recently published foreword by replacing the architectonic and hierarchical metaphors "building," "cornerstone," "foundation," etc., with "network" metaphors – a fact which is, however, of no consequence for our investigation. See Lutz, 1984, 8.

26. Gregory Bateson, *Steps to an Ecology of Mind* (New York: Ballantine Books, 1978); Bateson, 1979, 173.

27. Marlis Gerhardt, "Über Macht und Ohnmacht," in Claudia Opitz, ed., *Weiblichkeit oder Feminismus?* (Weingarten, 1984); Ferguson, 1987, 227.

28. See Opitz.

8. The Feminization of Society

1. Erwin Chargaff, *Warnungstafeln – Die Vergangenheit spricht zur Gegenwart* (Stuttgart, 1982), 237.

2. Alfred Mechterseimer, ed., *Nachrüsten? Dokumente und Positionen zum NATO-Doppelbeschluss* (Reinbek bei Hamburg, 1981), 19.

3. Roger Garaudy, *Pour l'avenement de la femme* (Paris: A. Michel, 1981).

4. Horst-Eberhard Richter, *Alle reden vom Frieden: Versuch einer paradoxen Intervention* (Reinbek bei Hamburg, 1981), 19.

5.   Cited in Friedrich Pasierbsky, *Krieg und Frieden in der Sprache* (Frankfurt, 1983), 141.

6.   Quoted in Elisabeth Brandle-Zeile, ed., *Seit 90 Jahren – Frauen für den Frieden* (Stuttgart, 1983), 23.

7.   Herbert Marcuse, in Silvia Bovenschen and Marianne Schuller, "Weiblichkeitsbilder: Interview mit Herbert Marcuse," reprinted in Jürgen Habermas and Silvia Bovenschen, eds., *Gespräche mit Marcuse* (Frankfurt, 1978), 75.

8.   See Brigitte Wartmann, ed., "Verdrängungen der Weiblichkeit aus der Geschichte," in *Weiblich-Männlich: Kulturgeschichtliche Spuren einer verdrängten Weiblichkeit* (Berlin, 1980), 7–33, and "Die Grammatik des Patriarchats: Zur 'Natur' des Weiblichen in der bürgerlichen Gesellschaft," in *Ästhetik und Kommunikation* 47 (Berlin, 1982): 12–32.

9.   Wilfried Gottschalch, *Geschlechterneid* (Berlin, 1984).

10.   Juliet Mitchell, *Psychoanalysis and Feminism* (New York: Random House, 1975).

11.   Gottschalch, *Geschlechterneid*, 45.

12.   Joachim-Ernst Berendt, *Das dritte Ohr: Vom Hören der Welt* (Reinbek bei Hamburg, 1985), 359, 327ff.

13.   Adrienne Rich, "Women and Honor: Some Notes on Lying," in *On Lies, Secrets, and Silence: Selected Prose, 1966–1978* (New York: Norton, 1979), 186.

14.   Jean-Paul Sartre, "Bad Faith and Falsehood," in *Being and Nothingness*, 89.

15.   Günther Anders, *Mensch ohne Welt* (Munich, 1964), introduction.

16.   See Jutta Brauckmann, *Die vergessene Wirklichkeit.*

9. Cross-Thinking / Counter-Questioning / Protest

1. "Frauenforschung oder Feministische Forschung?" *Beiträge zur feministischen Theorie und Praxis* 11 (1984): 5.

2. Erwin Chargaff, *Unbegriefliches Geheimnis: Wissenschaft als Kampf für und gegen die Natur* (Stuttgart, 1981), 225; *Warnungstafeln: Die Vergangenheit spricht zur Gegenwart* (Stuttgart, 1982), 249, 252, 248.

3. Chargaff, *No Serious Questions.*

4. Maria Mies, "Methodische Postulate zur Frauenforschung," *Beiträge zur feministischen Theorie und Praxis,* 1 (1978): 41–63.

5. Ilse Frapan, *Wir Frauen haben kein Vaterland: Monologe einer Fledermaus* (Berlin, 1983), first published in 1899.

6. See Günther Anders, *Hiroshima ist überall* (Munich, 1982).

7. See ibid., xxxii.

10. The Prohibition of Hatred

1. Volker Elis Pilgrim, "Wuthass, Neidhass, Leibhass," in Renate Kahle et al., eds., *Hass: Die Macht eines unerwünschten Gefühls* (Reinbek bei Hamburg, 1985), 82.

2. Klaus Trappmann, ed., *Landstrass, Kunden, Vagabunden: Gregor Grogs Liga der Heimatlosen* (Berlin, 1980), 224.

3. Dorothee Sölle, "Gibt es einen kreativen Hass?" in H. E. Bahr, ed., *Politisierung des Alltags* (Darmstadt: Neuwied, 1972), 254, 255.

4. See Günther Anders, *Hiroshima ist überall* (Munich, 1982).

5. Günther Anders, "Die Antiquiertheit des Hassens," in Renate Kahle et al., *Hass,* 11, 32.

6. Manfred Pohlen, "Die Vernichtung des Individuellen in einer 'befriedeten' Gesellschaft," in ibid., 260.

7. Cora Stephan, "Mit Entsetzen: Scherz," in ibid., 40.

8. See Jutta Brauckmann, *Die vergessene Wirklichkeit* (Münster, 1984).

9. Margarete Mitscherlich, *Die friedfertige Frau* (Frankfurt, 1985).

10. Friedrich Nietzsche, *Beyond Good and Evil: Prelude to a Philosophy of the Future,* trans. Walter Kaufmann (New York: Random House, 1966), 163–64.

11. Paul J. Möbius, *Über den physiologischen Schwachsinn des Weibes* (Halle, 1907).

11. The "Moral Insanity" of Women

1. Ann Jones, *Women Who Kill* (New York: Fawcett, 1981).

2. "GAU – die Havarie der Expertenkultur," *Kursbuch 85* (Berlin, 1986).

3. Eberhard Jens, "Am aussersten Rand," in ibid.

4. Claudia von Werlhof, "Wir werden das Leben unserer Kinder . . ." in Marina Gabaroff et al., *Tchernobyl hat unser Leben verandert: Vom Ausstieg der Frauen* (Reinbek bei Hamburg, 1986), 8–24.